Franklin D. Israel

to my mother and father, I dedicate this book

Franklin D. Israel

buildings + projects

introduction by Frank O. Gehry   essays by Thomas S. Hines and Franklin D. Israel

Rizzoli NEW YORK

First published in the United States of America in 1992
by Rizzoli International Publications, Inc.
300 Park Avenue South, New York, NY 10010

Library of Congress Cataloging-in-Publication Data

Hines, Thomas S.
Franklin D. Israel : buildings and projects : essays /
by Thomas S. Hines, Franklin D. Israel ; introductionby
Frank O. Gehry.
p. cm.
Includes bibliographical references.
ISBN 0-8478-1538-2 (hc)
1. Israel, Franklin D. 2. Architecture, Modern—20th
century—United States. I. Israel, Franklin D. II. Title.
NA737.I786A4 1992   91-52885
720'.92—dc20   CIP

Designed by Tracey Shiffman of
Shiffman/Young Design Group

Edited by Joe Day and Dan Waterman

Front cover: photograph by Tom Bonner, detail,
Tisch-Avnet
Background texture on front and back cover taken from
Tisch-Avnet, interior walls, photographs by Tom Bonner.

Back cover : Drawing from the Woo Pavilion.

Printed and bound in Singapore
Reprinted in 1997

contents

above: *detail*, UCLA Installation II

page 1: *detail*, Gillette bath
page 4: *detail*, Altman handrail

acknowledgments

I would like to acknowledge the following people for their support, assistance, and encouragement during the time spent putting this publication together. I am grateful to Joe Day for his thoughtful and sensitive editing, at times imbued with sweeps of brilliance. I bow to Tracey Shiffman, Japanese style, for her talents, visual insights, and deep commitment to the design of this project. Richard Weinstein, Herbert Muschamp, Aaron Betsky, Jaquelin Robertson, Julia Bloomfield, Carol Vogel, Jim Van Scoyoc, and my old friend Suzanne Stephens have consistently inspired me with their helpful criticism and friendly persuasion. I would also like to acknowledge Philip Johnson and Frank Gehry, whose interest in and criticism of my work have always served to improve it and to make it more contemporary, more Californian. Without their encouragement, this book would still lie dormant, in many pieces around the city.

Other friends—Roz, Mary Lambert, the Goldsmiths, Harriet Gold, Sarah Novack, Terry Bissell, Steve Saletan, Paul Fortune, Bernie Frischer, Jo Wilder, Philip Smith, David James, Lee Brevard, and Kamal Kozah—have listened to my angst about keeping things afloat.

Mostly, I wish to acknowledge the many people with whom I have worked and whose efforts fill this volume. Steven Shortridge, Barbara Callas, Annie Chu, Tom Rael, Jeffrey Chusid, Mitchell DeJarnet, Rick Gooding, Jay Deguchi, Leslie Shapiro, Milena Iancovici Murdoch, Danielle Guthrie, and Danny Kaplan are a few of the many who have contributed to the work. Many were students of mine at UCLA, where we first started to learn and design together. I'd also like to recognize Grant Mudford and Tom Bonner, whose beautiful photographs have consistently documented my work in a clear and comprehensive way. The craftsmanship of Steve Foster and Ed Burnell have added much to the realization of these buildings.

Finally, I bow to my clients: Andrea Rich, Marisa Arango, Bill Berry, Howard Goldberg, Jim Bean, Fred Weisman, Keith Bright, Steve Tisch, Jon Avnet, Jeff Ayroff and Jordan Harris, Simon Fields, Steve Golin, Joni Sighvatsson, Randy and Diane Roberts, Joel Grey, Jo Wilder, Michele Lamy, Richard Newton, Robert and Kathryn Altman, Rick Gillette, Philip and Ida Snell, Michael Woo, Susan Fong, Sydney and Susan Baldwin, and the Kaplans. These women and men ultimately make it all possible—they prefigure the work, and it is a testimony to them.

In this respect, I would like to underscore two of my most challenging and stimulating patrons, David Bombyk and Jay Jinkins, who have passed away. Their vivid imagination and provocative criticism proved a turning point in the development of my work. I salute David as a great friend and human being whose sense of dignity and purpose infused every effort he applied himself to, including the house we designed together but were not able to build.

The projects and photographs included here are mementos of a particular time and place. I hope they signal something better, inspiring understanding as well as a good amount of fun. We did have fun doing this work.

Frank O. Gehry

Frank Israel and I met about twelve years ago at my office in Santa Monica. I used to give slide shows of our work in progress, and Philip Johnson brought Frank by to see what we were doing. These were pretty regular occasions then, and we tried to get as many people to take a look as we could. Philip was always trying to bring different talents together to see what sparks flew, and he had met Frank Israel in New York putting together the "Forty under 40" show.

When we met, Frank was still really interested in set design and had worked at Paramount to see what that industry was about. Architecture seemed closer to his heart, though. For someone just out of New York, he seemed pretty relaxed and open to what was going on around him. He did return to architecture, as this book and his many fine buildings confirm, and we became close friends over the years. As is the case with most people that live close to their calling, one can learn much about the man from his work.

I recently got to see the addition Frank did for Michele Lamy and her family, and at every level this little pavilion reveals Frank's talent. Though from the street the addition just peeks out over the existing house, the project eclipses the original, giving it an identity and resonance that weren't hinted at before. As you move through the happenstance spaces of the old residence, you hit Frank's studio, and you wonder where the heart of this house could have been before his addition.

The studio gives the Lamy-Newtons a clear, open space to inhabit as they see fit; the pavilion gives the neigborhood a completely new presence. Monumental and pristine, the cube of the pavilion contrasts with the scale and geometry of every building in the area, but without offense. As in all of Frank's work, the deep tonal colors warm the space and reinforce the design. This project masters the subtle art of improving circumstances without completely submitting to them.

Frank set his pavilion off from, but adjacent to, the original. He then imposed formal limitations on himself that most architects would chafe under. The pavilion is the most dignified object-building on the street, yet it is hidden and facing backwards. By composing the rear of this house so carefully, Frank showed how tired the stylized fronts of most of the surrounding homes are. He managed to invert the standard banalities and polite asymmetries of the neighborhood.

In the Lamy-Newton addition, a set of red sliding doors open toward the pool. Both of the delicate red doorframes are reinforced with cables and turnbuckles, and each holds a single expanse of sandblasted glass. Though they may refer to some industrial example, these doors have been crafted to minute specifications to fit this design as they do. They establish, or at least reveal, the proportional meter of the whole pavilion. The character of the project, formal and experiential, hinges on the opening and closing of those doors. When the doors are open, the rear wall of the pavilion pulls away to become a checkerboard of red and yellow planes. When closed, the facade pulls back to form an inscrutable face—the banded eyes and Schindler ears are open, but the mouth is firmly shut.

Symmetry, modular proportions, anthropomorphic forms: these comprise a classical architecture, but revamped and retooled into something groundbreaking. Frank realizes that the hopes and aspirations of his clients are the most precious assets of an architect. Here, he made a living space for the Lamy-Newtons out of their own enthusiasm for life, adventure, and transgression.

Over the years I have been approached by a few people in the entertainment business looking for residential architects. I'm often leery of working with people in the "industry" because I generally have a pretty clear idea of what I want a project to become, and often they do as well. When Jo Wilder and Joel Grey came to me looking for someone to design their home, I had two conflicting thoughts: these were interesting, high-powered people, but these were interesting, high-powered people that already had a very personal vision of what they wanted out of their home.

Maybe because he didn't grow up around film and television production, Frank may have a more romantic idea of the "imagemaker" in Hollywood than I do. At any rate, he has a real gift for transforming the imaginings of moviemakers into beautiful buildings that reflect both his vision and theirs. He loves seeing the world through the eyes of others. Frank worked with the Grey-Wilders on two designs, and after both, they thanked me for recommending him. When people in the performing arts ask me for advice, I invariably include Frank Israel among my recommendations. Though he works for a lot of different people on a lot of different projects, Frank deals better with "stars" than anyone else in town.

A few years after working with the Grey-Wilders, Frank was commissioned to design an addition to a building of mine, the Mid-Atlantic Toyota complex in Maryland. Though the scheme didn't get built, it would have dramatically altered—and dramatically added to—the original. His addition wraps around the existing building, giving it a completely new streetside facade. It was a very mixed program, all to be contained in a strip along the outer wall of the existing structure. His design was to include administrative offices, and showrooms for the cars and art that the company had purchased. Frank's solution was really beautiful. He created a scheme that had an intense internal rhythm and exterior development that both respected and pulled away from what I had done. The larger complex would have fit its site more sensitively than I had been able to manage within the constraints of the original commission.

Some of Frank's successes with demanding clients stem from his disarming charm and enthusiasm; part follows from his gift for matching their creativity with his own; still more has to do with his clarity and exactitude in design. In the end, clients get a building that is more expressive, more inclusive, and more well-reasoned than they asked for. There is an easy grace to Frank's buildings, but also a tight, thorough attention to detail.

Once he understands what he needs to do, Frank is pretty conscious about how his raw material will translate into built form. With his training and his prodigious memory, Frank seems much more secure with pulling historical reference into his work than do many other architects in the city. When he plays on a window from Schindler, for example, Frank knows the source he's drawing from, and he understands how his work can be informed by that of others without being constrained by their model.

He was mature on arrival from New York. Beyond his education, Frank had experience in planning and city government. He was attuned to the sensibilities of New York and probably never ran into the condescension that West Coast designers sometimes meet in the East. Though he seems pretty comfortable bridging the two cultures, he seems to fit best here. Frank has enough ties with the East to demystify and understand where he came from.

Frank and I have a lot of common ground. Both of us absorb our surroundings, recast what we see, and examine how those realities impact on the human psyche. Our visions don't exactly coincide, and I hope he holds to his own. A lot of the younger designers—Morphosis, Eric Owen Moss, and others—have very personal visions of how buildings come together. I worry that with the exposure and pressure of reductive catchalls like the "New LA School," they have started to converge in dangerous ways. At the moment, more than a few of the best LA designers seem heavily under the influence of Carlo Scarpa, for example. I hope they can keep their distance from one another.

I've been asked how I influence younger architects, and I think I have impacted on these designers, but not in the ways people generally tie architects together. Most of the ways are as much material as philosophical. In Los Angeles, there aren't many precedents in the built environment—no cornice lines, no brownstones, no monumentalized areas that have to be respected and acknowledged. In this context, small jobs can be taken as seriously as large ones, and celebrated in a way that they aren't in most places. Additions like the Lamy pavilion can take on a life of their own and foster urban orders no less viable than those of the buildings they accompany.

I try to take small jobs really seriously, even after completing many larger projects. It seems that there are freedoms at a moderate scale that can lead to new discoveries in my work. You can, for instance, employ a greater range of materials without being too precious. You can try different things until forms come together in harmony and in dissonance, and you can alter the pitch of either. I think I've passed this lesson along to the people I work with and to others in the city.

Unfortunately, many designers now have no choice but to work on small-scale commissions at the moment. Until the economy improves, and maybe even after it does, the West Coast is going to be the place where the most innovative work will happen. Whether he learned it from me or someone else, Frank Israel makes the most out of every commission he takes on. He's done some big projects now, and he approaches them with the same hunger he does his residential work. I hope over the next decade Frank gets the opportunity to do some major public buildings because he is ready for it. He has the vision, the responsibility, and the skill to take on any scale. With luck and an upswing in the economy, we will live with more and more of Frank's work.

On another level, Frank has already changed the face of the city dramatically. By more accounts than just my own, he is the strongest force at work right now in design at UCLA, and one of the strongest teaching voices in Los Angeles over the last decade. He draws critics and students to the school, and his studios consistently represent the best design work going on in the city. Unlike many architects that have difficulty moving from their own work to that of others, Frank sees his students' work as they themselves do and tries to improve their thinking from within their own systems of logic.

It's this compassion that pulls Frank away from his contemporaries and that makes him a consummate architect. He is generous with his wisdom and his talents. With his students, as with his clients and associates, Frank has incredible empathy. Their condition becomes his own, but with the distance of perspective that allows Frank to place their needs and aspirations to greater advantage than they could alone. There is a human quality to his work that could only derive from a deep understanding of, and a deep concern for, the people around him. Where others have pulled abstractions out of the sky to justify their designs, Frank has grounded his work in the realities of human necessity and desire. By being open to these needs and aspirations, rather than running from them, Frank has found powerful inspiration and unique directions for his own work.

Through this brand of humanism,   **we all benefit**

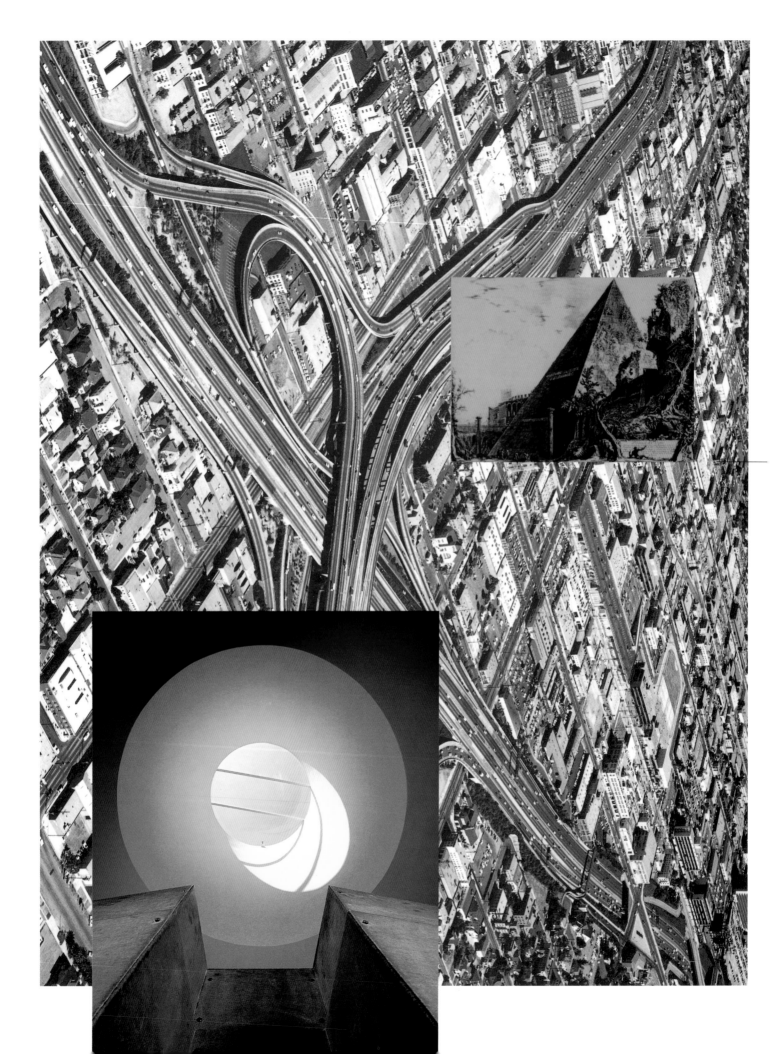

cities within

Franklin D. Israel

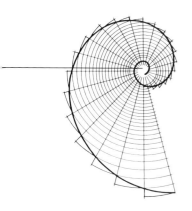

facing page:
Top inset: Piranesi's drawing of Pyramid of Cestius
Background: View of freeway in Los Angeles
Bottom inset: Oculus at Tisch-Avnet

Almost all architectural debate today takes place relative to a notion of the city, or at least a notion of *some* city. Yet, the city I work in, Los Angeles, can be summed up thoroughly only in terms of its elusiveness. Biographers of the city have sought in vain to define the hard and fast "character" of Los Angeles. Most have found solace only in her outskirts: the desert, the mountains, and the coastline, all of which begin to offer identifiable, though now hardly immutable, confines to the human phenomena comprising Los Angeles. Banham, Soja, Baudrillard, and Davis—to name a few critics—all began studies of urban Los Angeles only to opt in the end for treatments of her periphery.

Margins, rather than centers, define Los Angeles. Margins define the percentage of profit and the scope of development; margins secure the protection of some and the exclusion of others; margins divide reality from the *unreal*, the *hyper-real*, and most recently, the *irreal*.[1] The sighting of these margins, necessarily as transient as the charting of high and low watermarks, remains the most objective route one can take to understanding the city. And even here things are prone to odd reversals of reason. How is one to design and build—acts so concrete—in an environment so fluid?

Some constants of the profession narrow my question a little; but again, in Los Angeles, very little. In any project, architects must come to terms with a client, a site, and a set of community standards for building. Each of these factors, as well as the formal strategies gleaned in my training in the East, play into my work, often in decisive ways. Yet "client" can take on a new, if not a contrary, meaning when one considers the median duration of a Californian marriage or the logic behind multimillion-dollar companies seeking a "young and reckless" edge. Across LA, community standards and building codes range from the near-nonexistent to the ferociously stringent. Finally, even the earth below our feet (or, as often, our tires) lacks the stability of other cities. Unless client, site, and context are engaged in an original way and until some relatively subjective layers are added to the situation, one sees each project as through a looking glass that inverts image and increases its distance as you near.

I hope to show in this essay, however, that much of my work is influenced positively by the nature of where I work, and that a dialogue can be established within the rare conditions encountered by Southern Californian designers. I would like to further argue that what one can learn from practicing in Los Angeles may contribute greatly to an understanding of how to build in any dynamic culture today. I hope that my designs included here offer a few directions of inquiry into this city, and into *the* city more generally. Before entering into a discussion of my work, however, I would like to pose a more personal reading of Los Angeles that has grown out my experience of a second city, Rome, where I lived at the American Academy from 1973 to 1975. The nature of both these places plays an important part in my designs.

Though noting a resemblance between two places may or may not yield fresh insight into either, more than a few analogies can be drawn between Los Angeles and Rome. It is clear that my built work, and my understanding of the urban environment more generally, owe much to the reflections and contrasts to be found between these two cities. The dialogue linking Rome and Los Angeles suggests in turn a conversant architecture, a method of design that speaks *with*—rather than strictly *to*—client, site, and circumstance.

To wade a little at the level of platitude, most comparisons of the two cities speak first of their affluence and ascendancy. Basking in a "Mediterranean" glow and producing more than her fair share of presidential (if not to say *imperial*) talent, Los Angeles may be the "new Rome" of the moment. With Tokyo close on our heels, Los Angeles may also prove a stepping stone in the westward trend of global culture theorized by today's "Pop" historians. Athens, Rome, Paris, London, New York, and now the Pacific Rim metropolises will each enjoy a stint as "throne-among-seats" of civilization, or so the argument runs.

One could as easily paint a comparison of Rome and Los Angeles in terms of diffusion, diversity, and decadence. Certainly both cities must be framed as crossroads as well as destinations. If "all roads lead to Rome," as many roads now depart from Los Angeles. On the distant fringes of their respective continents, Rome and Los Angeles are both final outposts of a dominant order and first havens to the newly enfranchised. Whether in the forms of bath houses and amusement parks, or in the figures of Caligula and Brett Easton Ellis, the two cities have periodically redefined luxury and dissolution as few locales have.

For the architect, however, the ties and divisions between Rome and Los Angeles carry more than a passing importance. Unlike most major Western cities in which *place* can be assigned relative to the old and once-cordoned village center, post-Renaissance Rome and contemporary Los Angeles find definition primarily relative to visions of nature and culture outside themselves. Those that seek a metropolitan nexus in either city are perennially disappointed or misled. Judging from Piranesi's etchings of a Roman *Il Campo Marzio*, or from the no-less-fictitious *Thomas Guide* to Los Angeles, the quandary is not that either city lacks figure in ground, but that in each city serial figuration has made the very notion of ground suspect.

Ruled by counterpoint and paradox, the aesthetic climate of Rome and Los Angeles must always be sought in the context of an *elsewhere*, rather than in an idealization of a centered, closed whole. In this sense, the cultures of the two cities follow patterns of development that I would term *dialogical*, as opposed to the more centrifugal pattern of other cities. Though I will refrain here, one could make a viable argument that the most telling similarities between Rome and Los Angeles lie in two macrogeographic parallels. Both cities find modern identity primarily relative to declining cultural centers to their east: Athens, in the case of Rome; New York, in the case of Los Angeles. To stretch the point, republican Rome and radical Los Angeles could each claim a kind of secondary polarity with more staid, refined, and aristocratic hamlets to their north—Venice and San Francisco, respectively.

But more important—or at least more approachable within the terms of this essay—are the manners in which Rome and Los Angeles and their inhabitants come to terms with the uniquely external focus of their economies and cultures. This is not to make the provincializing argument that either city can be written off as "superficial" in its preoccupations. Both the Rome of Piranesi's time and the Los Angeles of today harbor more than their fair share of literate and creative genius. But split between the Academy and the Vatican then, or between the movie studios and the military-industrial complex now, the cultural voice of both cities can be heard only in many small outbursts. In a climate where all parties speak and none listen, the architect is left the Herculean task of placement, as opposed to the Promethean role of mere inspiration. Meaning need not be created in Los Angeles. It must be extracted from the many conversations that already exist, and set off so that—however briefly, and for however large or small an audience—a coherent message is carried.

Perhaps this analogy between Rome and Los Angeles is overdrawn. The two cities are obviously very different. Buildings are sited differently in Los Angeles than they are in Rome. In LA they crop up, whereas in Rome they seem to be layered and imbedded in the terrain. This can partly be explained by the geological and topographical differences between the two cities. In Rome buildings can be physically encrusted into the landscape. But in LA, where the soil conditions are very poor and the risk of earthquakes constantly high, buildings tend to have a more ephemeral quality. The houses that are situated in the LA hills seem to hover above the ground like machines from another world, a constant reminder that Los Angeles, as a place, is not destined to exist without the mammoth, willful exertion of man.

Not only do the two cities differ in regard to the physical landscape in which they are situated, but also in regard to the societies which spawned them. The needs, desires, and ideologies of Rome—first an imperial seat of government, then the temporal capitol of a spiritual power, and finally the center of a nineteenth-century nation–state—differ from the ambitions of a vibrant, commercially oriented conurbation on the Southern California coast. Though perhaps less consolidated than most European cities, Rome is, and always was, a much more unified whole than LA, which is made of hundreds of distinct, enclosed entities: shopping malls, cineplex centers, film studios, and urban villages. Each is separated from the others by the barriers of freeways and garden streets. Elements such as the freeway are an integral part of the life force of Los Angeles. On one level, the freeway appears to serve the same function as the Roman street, a way of moving from one point to another. But unlike the unifying nature of the Italian street, the freeway can also be seen as a vehicle of escape, something which really cannot be attributed to its Roman counterpart, unless you consider the aqueduct an equivalent tributary.

It could be argued that in LA there is a more introspective atmosphere; its residents want a self-contained living and work space divorced from the reality they see existing in the modern world around them. Smog-filled air, traffic at a standstill, and an increasing perception of horrifying violence have all served to reinforce the idea that the "real" world is something to escape from. Architects must respond to these fears and offer solutions that help the anxieties of all people. Fear of the modern world and ways to conquer that fear are themes which

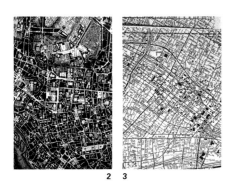

2 3

4

1 View of houses in Hollywood Hills
2 Nolli map of Rome
3 Thomas Guide to Los Angeles
4 View of Roman Forum with Vittorio Emmanuele
   Monument in distance
5 The "garden" at Santa Monica & Vine
6 *Sketch*, car, for the film "Autoroma"

run through most of my work, at times subtly, at other times more evidently.

Los Angeles proclaims itself as the ultimate modern phenomenon; the open, free, and extroverted modernist experiment brought to life. It was to be a city of promise, good fortune, and myth-making. Fear, anxiety, and introspection were not envisaged by the planners in the first half of the century. They could foresee, however, the tremendous eclectic building explosion of the postwar years as separate towns grew together into a giant potpourri of urban villages. The nearest equivalent to this phenomenon is New York of the early twentieth century, a city in which foreign styles and rituals were imported *en masse* and used unashamedly in the architecture. A similar radical eclecticism is evident in LA, though without New York's grid to unify its diverse styles. It exhibits a wonderful cornucopia of imported influences, some good, some bad, but all helping to create a synergistic energy that infuses all the work. I am attracted by this process and its results, and have tried to incorporate in my work the remnants of this creative energy.

There is a garden near my house in LA which I pass every day when I go to the gas station to fill up my automobile. It is an important garden to me, reflecting an eclectic attitude and a mosaic of influences. It is made of astroturf, and in this little piece of vibrant artificiality can be found much of the underlying philosophy of LA: the blatant import of images, in this case eternally green grass, has been a necessity in order to re-create the reality that the beholder wants to see.

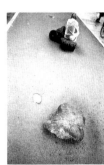

5

As it unfolds, this comparison reveals a kind of opportune reasoning. I do not compare one city to another to achieve a "balanced" comprehension of both, but to locate myself in the present. The Rome of antiquity, the Rome of my memory, and the Rome of this argument may or may not ever overlap with the Rome of today. If these Romes ever coincide with one another or with Los Angeles, they do so only within the imagination, as "cities within." I offer the above ruminations as some indication of how I orient myself to my surroundings. Comparing Los Angeles to Rome, New York, or elsewhere gives me some plausible counterpoint by which to judge my decisions and impact on this city. To cut short this internal dialogue, and to turn now to its implications for my designs, I would like to extract a few thematic observations and illustrate these points with specific examples from my work.

When called upon to explain my design work, I have divided my discussions into six themes. These, in turn, could be considered as three pairings. *Cities Within* and *Perpetuating Traditions* orient my work toward the city at the most general level, proposing a method of urban analogy in design in the first, and a method of social engagement in the second. The second pair of themes, *Origins and Order* and *Found and Borrowed*, work at a more microcosmic level. *Origins and Order* maps out the formal conventions that lend internal order to individual works, taking a kind of abstracted bird's-eye view of my work within the cityscape. *Found and Borrowed* focuses on the role of symbol and signage in my buildings, or as I put it earlier, extracting meaning from the conversations of Los Angeleno culture. Finally, *Pavilion in a Garden* and *Shaped and Bodied* explore two attitudes I've taken toward building outside an urban milieu, but within the inescapable consciousness of the city.

6

1.1 cities within

As may be apparent by now, myths of community-building ground many of my projects. Though I would grant LA a greater sense of urbanity than would many of her more acerbic critics, one can't help but enter into many projects here with the sense that a more human scale and closure is needed. As many of my larger commissions to date have asked for the rearticulation of interior spaces, I have had the opportunity to develop a number of tactics for rescaling existing environments to a variety of ends. Diagrammatic in this regard is an installation of mine constructed for the Walker Art Center in Minneapolis. The exhibit neatly encompassed many of the themes of my work, and leads easily into a later discussion of the "internal villages" designed for Propaganda Films, Bright and Associates, and Virgin Records.

The show consisted of six minimal wooden pieces—pavilions— arranged in a room, each one for the display of my work. The display panels were made of a material resembling concrete called glaswal, and they were then hooked onto the wooden frames by a series of steel clips. In essence, the wooden pavilions became scaffolding on which to hang ideas. Each one represented a different form of structure and architectural pattern, each grid announcing a vitality of construction and a potential for different forms.

They became a framework in which to locate fragments of an industrial and mass-media

7 8

9 10

vernacular language which, in turn, stands against the abstract backdrop of the sea, desert, mountains, and freeways of LA. I used this technique of montage, collage, and broken narrative to emphasize a whole range of stylistic diversity. I also wanted to express a sensual handling of materials as well as a certain sense of theatricality. (When I first arrived in LA, I did some work as a set designer before becoming, like so many before me, disillusioned with the industry.) Lastly, I wanted to visualize these feelings of refuge and the need to escape that I have mentioned above.

Five of the six pavilions allowed the viewer to enter and surround himself with the installation. The sixth, however, did not. It consisted of six live pine trees placed within the protection of one of the pavilions; the viewer could touch the trees only through the wooden slats. Here, I wished to express the idea of a refuge, a "safe oasis" which the spectator was prevented from fully entering. The viewer was kept at a distance; he could perceive the idealized world of trees but was prevented from fully being a part of it.

The overarching metaphor of the reincapsulated city finds its way into almost all of my work, and points to a conclusion drawn by Joseph Rykwert in *The Idea of a Town*, a study of the origins of Rome:

> Urban man is exposed not only to the personal predicament, but to that of the social personality, of the society to which he belongs as a person: a person androgenously incarnate in the city founder and its unknown protecting deity. It is this person which is guarded against the dangers inherent in the urban situation by the powerful defences of which I have spoken; the individual was guarded against it even more powerfully in prehistoric times, by the regenerative and reconciling pattern of the town itself.[2]

1.2 perpetuating traditions

Insofar as my work addresses an existing urban fabric, it also addresses the history of its place and the people responsible for that history. I take the social art of architecture seriously, both in terms of engaging a client in the act of building, and in reconciling my designs with surroundings and precedent. As I have designed primarily for sites in Southern California, I am drawn to the examples of early Californian modernists, and to "Mediterranean" modernism more generally. Often my concern and respect for this tradition is mirrored in the people I work with, as when clients supply me with sources that they would like to explore. The clients in the visual arts are often the best informed and most forceful in this regard. Such was the case in two of my more collaborative efforts, the Gillette Studio and the Altman House.

Contrary in terms of its location, but representative in many other respects, the Gillette Studio was a renovation of a loft in New York City which I did while living in Los Angeles. The site consisted of the boiler room at the top of the Liberty Tower, a building in lower Manhattan built in 1929. At that time, the client worked as a hair and makeup artist in the fashion business (he is now a photographer). He wanted to create a place in which to both live and work. Once the space was demolished, we gave it a rigid formal structure uniting the project as a whole. From the front door, a major axis follows, past the electrical and security systems into a vestibule area where the client intended to set two major objets d'art. This axis continues into the major studio space beyond. As if in a ritualistic procession, the visitor is unconsciously propelled through a series of frames and gates.

Visually, one may discern some references to the work of Luis Barragán. This was due to an interest my client had in Barragán's work after he had returned from a business trip to Mexico. He was in love with Barragán and demanded that we use particular pieces, which we did. You can see the references quite clearly, in the staircase without railings that does not really go anywhere (except to a closet), or in the shower spout and jacuzzi pool where the water continually circulates from shower to jacuzzi, overflowing, only to start its cycle again. I enjoyed the irony that this Barragán-inspired interior landscape is thirty-one stories up in the air. A disaster can happen when it leaks, as it has a couple of times.

The juxtapositions in this project became pastiche. The project as a whole does not depend on them. In fact, some of the materials and colors have since changed. Today the client no longer likes Barragán, but prefers the Arts and Crafts movement. He has covered the concrete floor with carpet, added upholstered walls, and painted the persimmon walls olive. It is a very strange place at the moment. Despite these superficial changes, the basic design and its formal organizational logic remain unchanged. The potential chaos of contemporary life has been imposed here with an order that comforts the visitor.

In hindsight, the Barragán references seem a superficial complement to an underlying and more flexible system of order below. A similar process of historical investigation followed at the Altman residence in Malibu, this time in the terms of Carlo Scarpa. A film director, Bob Altman is an extremely creative and energetic man. The Altmans had purchased a beachfront home in danger of imminent destruction from both surf and landslides. He had been told, in fact, that the whole area could someday slide into the sea. But Bob is a real trooper. He approached me with a model, built with his son Matthew, of what they would like to do with the property.

To come to terms with two relatively novel conditions—the presumed impermanence of this home and the decisive acts already proposed by the model—I looked at examples of modern design produced within strict economic and environmental parameters. As I have before and since, I turned to the work of Carlo Scarpa, especially his Gavina shop in Bologna, of 1961. Though faced with very different obstacles, I found inspiration for dealing with the constraints of this project in Scarpa's response to the challenges of limited resources when building in postwar Italy.

The existing home was divided on two floors, and broken up diagonally into little nondescript rooms. He and his wife Kathryn wanted one very large loftlike space. To accomplish this, we gutted the entire lower floor, creating a series of different levels with no walls to separate the particular spaces. Creating a large vertical light well or interior court, we linked the first and second floors. Without resorting to walled partitions, the program was parceled out across the two open fields of the first and second floors, with a stairwell and light well joining the two and focusing the whole.

Here the references to Scarpa were perhaps less contrived and more "elemental" than those to Barragán in the Gillette project. There, motifs from Barragán were imported and refitted at a dramatic remove from their Mexican models, while many similarities of scale, climate, and locale connect the Altman renovation to the interior work of Scarpa. Here, as elsewhere, I joined in the nautical romanticism of Scarpa and earlier modernists. Within a fixed space and a predetermined strategy for the alteration of that space, I decided to "clear the decks" of the beach house and concentrate on chosen dramatic moments. Though clearly at different crossroads of human circumstance, the Altman residence and some of Scarpa's early apartment renovations share a sense of sensual domestic composition within larger spatial frames. In Scarpa's work and in mine here, one understands space "layered" at scales both grand and minute.

In other instances, I've paid small homages to local talents and masterpieces. This can be seen in a simple and direct way in the details of the Lamy-Newton House, which I will discuss more later. Schindler is recalled in the window design, and around the pool we used tiles and other bric-a-brac from the client's childhood home in France which are a direct reference to the Watts Towers in Los Angeles, themselves an amazing mixture of influences and materials. In a city so often accused of lacking, if not negating, history, I consider part of the challenge of designing here the exploration of a past that few care to recollect, a past excavated from the debris of the present.

2.1 origins and order

Though historical allusion may begin to *place* a building from without, more is required within. Memory, and the creation of memorable spatial patterns, also depend on a sense of program and signification.

When confronted with the sometimes daunting list of space usages for an entertainment company or even for a large residence, I turn to a number of formal conventions that order the environments we create. Inserted into each project, a series of common operations provide a readable and understandable language of composition. Formal conventions have always run through my work. When I tried to delineate a difference between what I was doing on the East Coast and my work here in LA, I felt that there were obvious differences. Later, though, I realized that the same language of composition ran through each project, in the East and the West, and tied the site, the program, and the character of the client together.

Though most of these relationships are discussed in the project descriptions for each

12

13

12 View of Rome
13 View of Los Angeles
14 Sunset Strip, Los Angeles
15 Vatican City
16 *Sketch*, Ostia Antica
17 Studies for Propaganda Films

work, Propaganda Films and Bright and Associates offer clear expositions of their range. Both projects are rooted in the task of understanding rather than in the imposition of a universal solution.

Propaganda Films is a small, young music video and film production company. They wanted me to turn a warehouse in Hollywood into their offices. The plan as it exists now is a series of conference rooms which are delineated as object pieces; a large central "boat" which floats in space containing executive offices, a series of auxiliary facilities, a film vault, financial offices, editing rooms, and spaces for creative directors. Naturally there is a screening room as well, and all these spaces are tied together by a major axis and subsidiary cross axes.

At first the client wanted an "office landscape" defined as a series of open partitioned spaces. I had just returned from a trip to Rome and during my visit there I had spent a day at Ostia Antica with Bernard Frischer, a classicist who guided me through the incredible ruins. What impressed me about this Roman town was its richly textured spaces and carefully articulated edifices. There were both object buildings and contextual pieces. The public spaces seemed to fall into these two categories as well. Because Propaganda Films was composed of a group of persons with distinctly different backgrounds and attitudes, I began to see the organization of the company in terms of an urban village, where serial spatial requirements could ground more "monumental" elements. The original design is a vaulted shell organized by a series of axes, along which the various components are aligned. The bow-string trusses which restrain the vault were projected in plan. This image was mirrored and the central office "boat" was made.

At Bright and Associates a similar approach was taken, though with more varied programmatic requirements and a greater concern for the "heritage" of the site. Located at 901 W. Washington Boulevard in Venice, the commission involved the renovation and transformation of three existing buildings into the identity and design offices for Keith Bright and Associates. This group of buildings, dating from 1929, served originally as a train shed, then a funeral parlor, and most recently as the offices of Charles and Ray Eames. The Eameses first occupied the premises in 1943.

The two larger brick buildings, previously connected by a small fire door, are now physically linked by a sheet-metal "tunnel." This tunnel is a major link in the entry sequence and disguises the transition from one building to the other. A two-story skylit atrium sits at the entry to the tunnel, surrounded by administrative facilities. This space is a parallelogram in plan and in section, derived from the irregular angles of the existing buildings. Outside, a steel-and-glass canopy defines the commencement of the dramatic entry sequence.

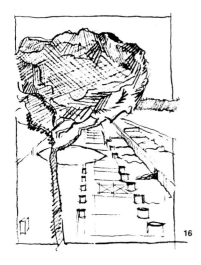

At the opposite end of the "tunnel," in the largest and oldest building on the site, lies an open multipurpose space dominated by an inverted cone sheathed in plywood, and containing a large conference room. Flanking this area are the executive offices. From this point adjacent facilities are arranged along a major longitudinal path that extends from this space to the east. One moves along this interior "street" past the executive design offices and the large design room, and into the production area. This axis is terminated by an obelisk demarcating the photo reproduction area, which is lighted from above. The obelisk refers to the Flatiron Building in New York, while the arcade of low arches recalls the subterranean vaulting of Grand Central Station and the Oyster Bar.

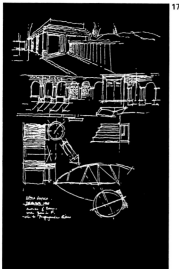

Outside, various sculptural objects have been placed strategically on the existing structures. These serve to link the group of buildings to its Venice context as well as to mark the location of the entrance, the fire stair, and the numerical building sign. These are constructed of steel, glass, and sheet metal. The interior atrium is visible as it pops up above the roof. The history of the site dictated a strategy in which much of the exterior was unchanged. When Charles Eames decided to paint portions of the exterior white, his decision was based on a belief that the reflections of the surrounding trees, telephone poles, and airplanes in the sky above were tantalizing moving portraits, appropriate visual statements of urban life. Our exterior attempts to update the Eameses' vision while providing Bright and Associates with a place they can call their own.

As in the Propaganda project, Bright and Associates depends on a number of clear and straightforward organizational tactics to mesh a vast array of concerns—from the nuts-and-bolts necessities of program to the incalculable spirits of the previous occupants. Though hardly unitary, these works create small but coherent "wholes" within the city—wholes that

18

19

20

21

build on, rather than pare from, one's understanding of the urban environment.

2.2 found and borrowed

Even in the most Spartan rendering of the polis, room must be left for play. As much as buildings should speak clearly when addressed, they should also shout and laugh, or whisper and cry, on occasion. Following the pattern of our spoken words, the voices that architecture might assume will inevitably borrow from surrounding idioms and syntax. But they need not only borrow from the languages of architecture. In sampling from movies, music, literature, and even the commercial and the discarded, we add daily to the richness of our communication. Following suit, architecture could speak volumes more than it does presently.

On two different occasions and for nearly opposite reasons, I have been confronted with promising, but at first seemingly "mute," commissions. Sited high in Beverly Hills with a staggering view of greater Los Angeles, the Arango-Berry House allowed only a remodeling and minor addition to a very standard, and very poorly sited, 1950s ranch house. Surrounded by a number of large and highly articulated office complexes (all designed by "signature" architects, in developer parlance), Virgin Records in Venice will be the first of these complexes to fall under new building codes that impose strict height and setback restrictions. In both instances, the confines of circumstance looked at first as though they might dramatically limit architectural expression. In both instances, however, limitations proved the springboard for successful design.

The Arango-Berry residence placed even greater hurdles before us than we first realized. Geological and structural considerations might have led the client to clear the site and build a new home, but we couldn't level the house due to limitations set by the grading regulations (which have since been lifted). Though the lines of the house had to be kept, new footings, flooring, and roof—essentially a new structural system—gave the interior a new and much-simplifed character. The interiors were stripped down to their 1950s frame. Views to the city were opened up by using very large picture windows and walls of transparent glass block. The cabinetry is pulled away from the original armature and revamped.

The original 1950s structure was completely gutted, the exterior scraped away, and new elevations designed. The overall composition is unified by a large overlaying roof which was rebuilt to enclose the heating, air conditioning, and ventilation ducts. The roof is covered in bonderized sheet metal. This material is also used on the addition which contains the master bathroom and dressing area. The pool was left untouched, and the brick deck around it extended to the new concrete steps and blue stucco garden wall. This wall is a major compositional element of the house; it links the garage to the front door, and is then brought inside following the entry gallery to the main living space. Much as an old book is reconstructed, rebound, and "artifacted" by a gifted archivist, our preservation of the existing house on the site delights in the act of repackaging, while holding to the form and format of the original.

After forcing music out of an object as unlikely as a tract house, we faced a more complex task in the case of Virgin Records. Though music was hardly lacking at the company, an architectonic cacophony screams along Main Street in Venice, where this project is sited. Few buildings within a quarter-mile of this site have *not* been built or redesigned within the last ten years by a high-profile LA architect. In addition to our relatively modest offices for Bright and Associates one block east, a multi-use complex by Jan van Tilberg stands to the north, capped off by a fifty-foot clown statue. Three blocks south at Windward Circle, no less than three monuments reflect the literal leanings of Steven Ehrlich. Perhaps most overwhelming of all, the collaborative effort of Frank Gehry and Claes Oldenburg for Chiat-Day—the Binocular Building—is our immediate neighbor.

To compound the difficulty of building for an image-savvy client in an image-saturated environment, the designs for Virgin would have to comply with new building ordinances that limit the facade of Virgin to approximately half the height of the Gehry project next door.

In response, we gambled on a design scheme of sophisticated and quiet resonance. Rather than present an acrobatic gesture that might quarrel with the "attitude" on display in either direction, Virgin remains aptly chaste and enigmatic. A carefully composed outer wall of steel, concrete, and sanded fiberglass shelters an inner domain of closed and open spaces, and provides an acoustic shield for Virgin's music-listening needs. Within, the building is divided so that meetings can be held—and music can be heard—in a variety of settings

18 Hollywood debris
19 Statue of Constantine, Campidoglio, Rome
20 Donut Shop: Inglewood
21 Bramante: Tempietto
22 Tail O' Pup, West Hollywood
23 Weisman Pavilion, construction shed
24 View of Los Angeles from Arango-Berry House

and at a variety of amplitudes. An innocent among the jaded, Virgin Records may have the last laugh. Though built elements could not exceed the twenty-foot height limit, hundreds of bamboo shoots in the fiberglass-clad entrance court should grow to well over seventy feet, offering welcome shade to the southerly offices of Chiat-Day. Though without the overt commercial clarity of other signs along Main Street, the "V" in Virgin is suggested in the reverse pitch of awnings over the front and rear entrances. A variety of gardens are interspersed throughout, allowing one space to contemplate the subtleties of the design or an early Sex Pistols release.

At the time of this writing, another scheme for Virgin has been planned, this time in Beverly Hills and next to the Geffen Record Offices designed by Gwathmey/Siegel. Beverly Hills and Venice share little more in common than the weather, and we worried about the change of site. But the Beverly Hills Architectural Review Board proved more intrigued with our work than I had anticipated. Though no longer sited among a number of daunting westside structures, the second scheme still reflects many of the lessons we learned from the first. Pared down in scale, but not in impact, the final design should engage its surroundings as concisely and effectively as the first.

3.1 pavilion in a garden

All of the projects I've discussed so far act directly within urban confines, except for the Arango-Berry House—which still takes many of its cues from a panoramic view of Los Angeles. A number of our houses and additions fall farther from the city, or at least are set in more active counterpoint to it. Hermetic and isolated, some of these projects can be seen as satirical "pavilions in a garden." The Lamy-Newton Pavilion and the Art Pavilion are both inward-looking and tightly ordered interventions in contrast to, rather than in harmony with, their surroundings.

In the first instance, a "pavilion in a garden" was the *least* confrontational strategy my client would support. Before alteration, the Lamy-Newton House, a "neo-Colonial" with rather banal features—sat innocuously in Hancock Park. The clients hated the house; they had moved there because of its proximity to their daughter's school. The client liked to consider himself avant-garde. One day he cut his front lawn with a machete in a severely expressionistic way and, not surprisingly, upset the neighbors. When he added several pairs of sacrificial sculptures, they became outraged.

We wanted to make this house a more liveable place, or at least a place that would "work" for him, his designer wife, and his family. When we began, they had just bought a book on Caribbean houses and they wanted to add a Caribbean front to the house with a thatched roof, but I refused. I felt the front of the house was adequate and it related well to its neighbors. It grounded the project in the existing context. Instead, we concentrated our work on the back of the building, adding a 730-foot steel-structured, two-story poolhouse/studio. In fact the space can serve as an art studio, gallery, guest bedroom, dining room, or just about anything else. But this isn't a mere addition. It is really a formal imposition to an existing nonformal house.

The house and addition are linked together into a cubistic composition. The studio manages to maintain a self-contained aloofness from the original home. Many of the elements used in the project are influenced by the work of Rudolph Schindler and Frank Lloyd Wright in California. The window details owe much to the work of these architects. In each case, they have been reinterpreted according to contemporary standards. The original details were fabricated in steel, which was less costly at the time. I modified them in wood, making them thicker and creating a great sense of juxtaposition with the columnar steel structure.

Upstairs, the master bedroom was enlarged by extending a deck which is accessed through double doors. The oak-clad balcony suspends over the entire space as a viewing platform for the client. It completes the axis which begins outside in the garden, ascending the pool steps onto the deck through symmetrically placed sliding doors. From this great perch, the clients can survey the scene. At a recent event, it provided a place for a group of gospel singers to do their thing while an audience listened below.

At another kind of remove stands the Art Pavilion. The project is a "freestanding" pavilion situated next to a large hillside home in Los Angeles, linked to the main house by a subterranean walk. The pavilion contains a large gallery and two floors for archives, guest lodging, and storage. A grounded "ark" for many species of contemporary art, the Art

25

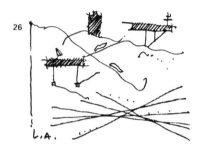

26

27

28

Pavilion presents the sheer, clean lines of a ship's outer hull, while revealing an almost nautical rigor within.

The pavilion is also a formal combination of Eastern and Western influences, employing both the monumentality and detailed construction of the Katsura Palace in Japan, while also acknowledging the prevailing Mediterranean style of Holmby Hills. The year before designing the building, I visited Katsura with a group of students and was struck by its symbiotic relationship with its landscape.

The Art Pavilion opens to a garden *below* as Katsura opens to a garden *outside*. A retaining wall pulls the pavilion into the hillside and rises further to give the building a formal "street" front, as opposed to its "garden" back. Though the exterior is unified by a stucco finish and tile roof, the building is a complex weave of trusses, frames, and inset panels that create more intimate "stage sets" for the work inside. Large corner windows also serve to bring in views of the trees and sky, while expanding on the references to Schindler and Wright from the Lamy-Newton House. A giant boat-shaped balcony hangs over the garden side of the building. Constructed of steel and wood, it will be covered with wisteria and bougainvillea. A smaller reference to the idea of an ark, it is intended to appear as if it were being raised to safety from the surging landscape below.

3.2 shaped and bodied

If the two additions just discussed work primarily as oppositional counterpoints to the datum of their surroundings, our most recent efforts attempt less contrary engagements of site and context. The Raznick, Kaplan, and Goldberg-Bean Houses are more comprehensive essays in non-urban form making than either the Lamy-Newton or Art Pavilion projects. Each required more in terms of program, and the Goldberg-Bean House faced an existing structure. Though the "freedom" to design homes on open and beautiful sites promised the thrill born of working on a tabula rasa, that freedom also called for a careful reassessment of designing without predetermined points of departure—or, at least, without the dense contexts of my previous work.

The Raznick and Kaplan projects follow two very different courses through the uncharted waters I imagined before me. Both, however, refer back to the dialogue that opened this essay. Though without the literalism of the large interior cityscapes at Propaganda and Bright and Associates, these residential projects also seek to reconstitute urban form in novel settings. Rather than becoming internal villages, these houses explore the psychological condition of removal from the city, and the methods by which we export cosmopolitan life.

The Raznick residence is a single-family home on a steep site in the Hollywood Hills of Los Angeles. The centerpoint of the arc which forms the house is located in the space formed by the wild canyon in which the house sits. The curved structure reaches out to engage the void, rather than the hillside.

The design thus allows the natural terrain and vegetation to move freely up the slope and among the piers which lift the residence. In addition, a fifth facade, the underside, is created and celebrated. The curve, in fact, echoes the dramatic landforms of the canyon (albeit in a rigorous way which makes clear its artificiality), and also pays homage to the movie industry by becoming a giant cinematic screen across which play the shadowed forms of the life within.

Along the street, the concave form of the house creates a plaza between the street wall so common in the Hollywood Hills, and the curved building. Upon entering this space, the visitor encounters a cistern waterfall—a traditional gesture of greeting in arid Los Angeles—immediately adjacent to the front door and aligned in composition with the requisite swimming pool.

The curve is not dominant in all realms: the roofscape is fragmented into separate forms over the living room, dining room, and master bath. A guest apartment sits above the garage, entered via the stair tower. This tower, the major vertical feature in the design, also visually anchors the building to the hillside.

The Kaplan residence is divided into two related wings on a site in the hills above the beaches of Malibu. Situated among native chaparral and wild grasses, the home is oriented toward the mountains and the sea: one complex for a writer, his two young sons, and professional wife; the other for his mother, a painter from Philadelphia.

Together the two sides of the residence enclose an elliptical courtyard, sited along an axis

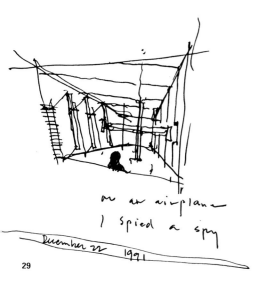

on an airplane
I spied a spy

December 22 1991

29

30

31

32

binding the mountains to the sea. The northern terminus of the axis is Point Dume, which also forms the northern tip of Santa Monica Bay. There is a 180° view of the ocean from the site. To preserve the spirit of the site and its sense of isolation, as well as to provide protection from the prevailing winds, the two homes are nestled into the slopes, and terraced with the site up to the north. As much of the site as possible is left untouched.

Two curving walls of concrete block shape the inner court and form the principal structure of both houses. These walls also define the structural and sculptural elements that form the home's living spaces. If the Art Pavilion offered an "ark" floating in a mountainous seascape, the Kaplan House might be best understood as the inverse. The two wings at the Kaplan residence surround a court that forms another ark, this time of void rather than substance.

conclusions

Predictably, as this is a book about my work, what began as a meditation on the urban present has veered into a discussion of my buildings and projects. This essay began in good faith: here, I would set forth my thoughts on a *conversant* architecture, and offer a philosophy of design by which others might benefit. A comparison of Los Angeles and Rome serves as a model of counterpoint by which I take in my surroundings and in turn contribute to them. Yet, as in the best of conversations, one cannot map out all of the paths that will be taken, nor even the end that will be reached. The transcendent moments in most conversations are exactly those that were not anticipated. In this sense, my designs argue my case more unexpectedly—and forcefully—than I do in words. As I've tried to subvert the boundaries between monument and metropolis in my designs, I have also tried to erode some of the distinctions between my polemic and my production.

Today, the architect must be a planner, builder, illusionist, diplomat, manager, employee, juggler, and psychiatrist, not to mention author. Architects do not have ultimate solutions anymore. We no longer have the same kind of confidence that our predecessors had in the early part of the century to offer answers and lay down plans for the future. We now realize that the control of the future is more difficult than we had presumed. But the past has always been able to provide us with directions. We can still realize our dreams, and we can still bring images and desires to fruition. But we have to show a greater awareness of, and a sensitivity to, the realities of contemporary life.

As Rome and Los Angeles compete to define my vision of the city, two composite images impact more and more on my designs for the city. The first is the changing metropolis itself. The second is another (perhaps *the* other) totality by which man has harnessed and prevailed over the forces of nature: the ship. The realm of the architect falls exactly between these two totalities, allowed neither the endless sprawl of the city, nor the closed perfection of the vessel at sea. But both ideals inform the many acts of building that bridge the two extremes. Architecture can embrace both urban plurality and nautical simplicity, streetwise rigor and seaborne repose. Perhaps more importantly, architecture orients man to nature and culture, both by representing the state of civilization at a digestible scale and by suggesting means of safe passage through the often-troubled waters of the present.

I would like to close with two images. The first is a plate from Piranesi's *Vedute di Roma*, a view of the Isle of Tiberina. The second is an interior view of the central office core at Propaganda Films. Though I've been flattered to have my work described as "Piranesian," this comparison is not intended to equate my vision with Piranesi's. Instead, I'm interested in what the two images say about modern city-making from exactly opposite historical perspectives.

Piranesi's etching pulls a few perspectival punches, streamlining a small island in the Tiber river into a form that presciently suggests an ocean liner of this century. From a prow of stone battlements, buildings mount the island after the tiered pattern of a ship's bridge. Miscellaneous pitched roofs reaffirm the central axis of the island/vessel, though they appear incidentally oriented to the structures they shelter. Two towers rise up: the larger could be the helm, the smaller a smokestack or perhaps a radar. Two delicately arched bridges tie the liner to the mooring of greater Rome. Though part of a larger and encroaching cityscape, Tibertina invents a new urban condition—both to act within the city *and* to pose an alternative to it.

The red core of Propaganda also recalls seafaring, as it informs the pattern of office space contained within its hull. No more and no less a vessel than Piranesi's island, the "boat" of

Propaganda splits the circulation of the office just as Tiberina divides the Tiber. However, the two ships rest at very different ports of call. Where all of Rome once served as ground to the Tiberina vessel, the ship of Propaganda rises and falls within an internal domain. The orthogonal boundaries of the preexisting structure at Propaganda resemble not the random parameters of Piranesi's Rome, but the rectangular borders that frame and contain his visions.

The first image poses an ominous future for heroic Tiberina, soon to be overwhelmed by greater Rome; the second depicts a redemptive response to the past, in which Propaganda wrestles a protective ark from the dense cityscape. The ubiquitous metropolis anticipated by Piranesi we can now view only with hindsight. Modern cities have grown to envelop and systematize all but the most secure and self-proclaiming of enclaves. However tentatively, we have already begun to reinhabit an overly rational world and tame its excesses. The task for future designers lies in repossessing the urban realm, and in taking the best work of today as the seeds of a more vital and human environment.

notes

1   For the uninitiated, "unreal" most often refers to surf conditions (very good); "hyper-real" connotes, for certain French cultural critics, the explosive urban expansion of the city and its attendant signage; "irreal" was recently coined by Margaret Crawford in *The Ecology of Fantasy* (Los Angeles: The Los Angeles Forum for Architecture and Urban Planning, Publication No. 3, 1988) to describe the thematized remodeling of Los Angeles after the models of Disneyland and other amusement parks.

2   Joseph Rykwert, *The Idea of a Town: The Anthropology of Urban Form in Rome, Italy and the Ancient World* (Boston: The MIT Press, 1989), 195.

facing page: *detail*, exterior plaster, Propaganda Films

buildings + projects

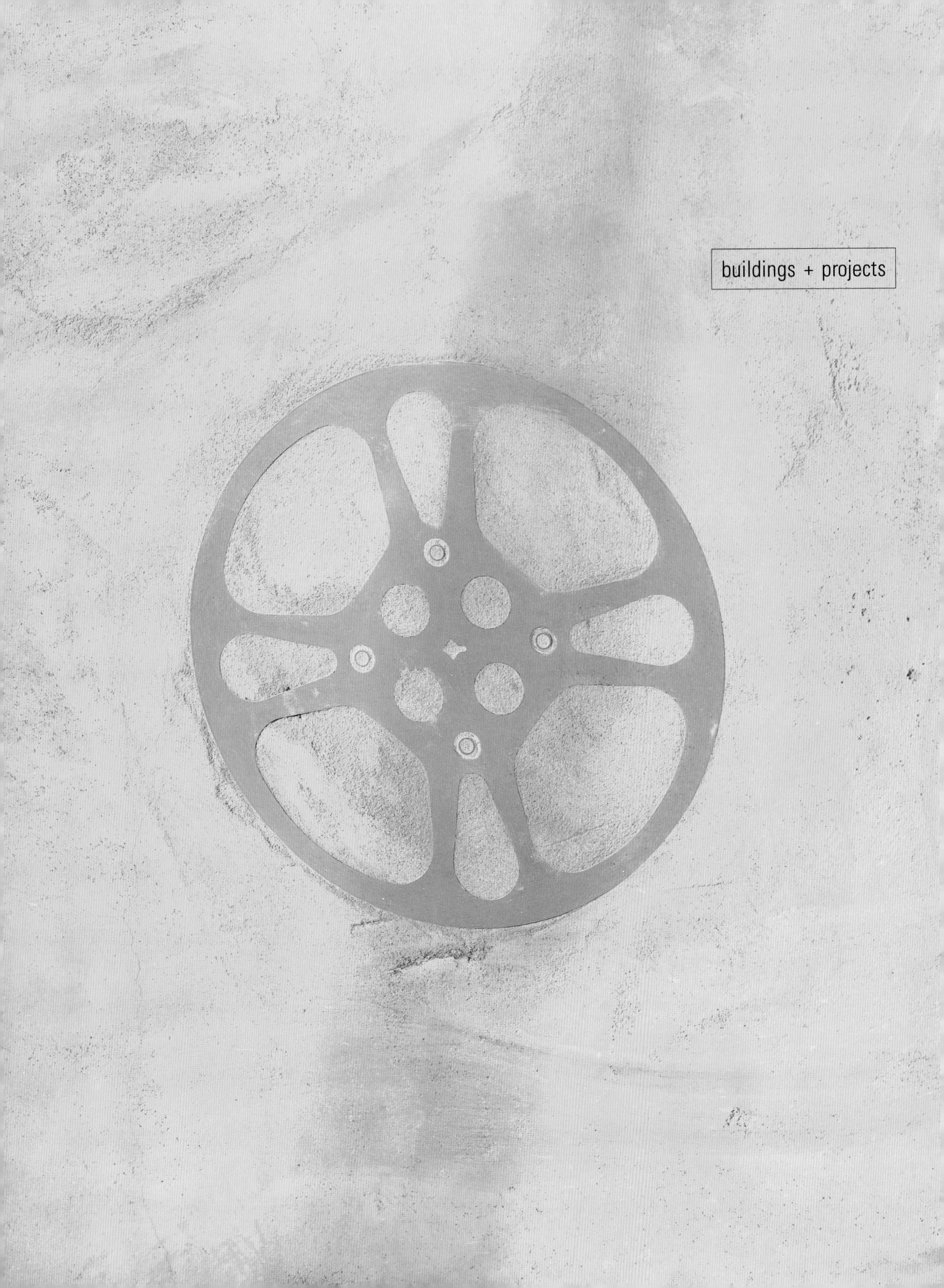

snell house

Amagansett, Long Island, New York   1972

The Snell House was my first professional commission. A seasonal home of 2,500 square feet, the residence was built at a very modest cost.

Located in the small seaside community of Amagansett on Long Island, the Snell House takes many of its cues from the surrounding architectural vernacular. Bedrooms on the first floor are oriented around a central hearth and allow each of the family members free access to the outdoors. Almost all the interior spaces have corresponding patios and verandas immediately adjacent.

Elements of the local shingle-style architecture have been streamlined and recombined to fill out a taut orthogonal frame. The tension between the modern and the traditional charges the design and reflects a formative theoretical position. Clad in siding and patterned after the logic of a specific regional architecture, the Snell House engages the history of its location, but at a clearly abstracted remove. Good sense, rather than sentimentality, guides the borrowings. Along the lines of the proverbial mousetrap, we set out to build a better "saltbox." Much of the detailing came out of on-site conversations with Jon Cavamegna, the contractor responsible for many of Charles Gwathmey's early homes.

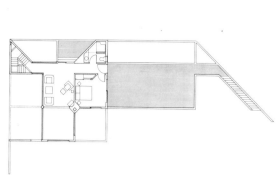

upper plan

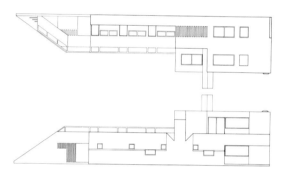

elevations

ground plan

view of exterior at 31st floor

gillette studio

New York, New York   1980–1982

A 3,000-square-foot living space for one in New York City, the Gillette Studio was completed in 1982. The studio reclaims the boiler room of a New York office tower, and transforms the vestigial space of the building into a living and working environment for a fashion photographer.

Once gutted, the space became a shell for a new, and in some ways foreign, pattern of order. The disparities of scale between this high, secluded retreat and the surrounding buildings of the

metropolis were accentuated by inversions of "civic" and "private" monumentality within the design itself. The ancillary needs of the client were clustered around the service core of stairwells and elevator shafts, leaving large open areas on either side. The concise planning of the kitchen, bath, and dining rooms complements the free and open studio and bedroom. In a more pointed juxtaposition, a miniature grand stairway leads up to a cubbyhole closet, while an oversized and ebullient bathtub overflows luxuriously in one corner of the living suite.

Transformations in the life of the client have led to many alterations of the original design, but the flexible overall pattern remains unchanged. At his request, we incorporated a number of clear references to the the work of Luis Barragán into the design. As Mr. Gillette's tastes moved away from Barragán and toward the motifs of the Arts and Crafts movement, the studio has taken on new character, but without sacrificing the essential structure of the whole.

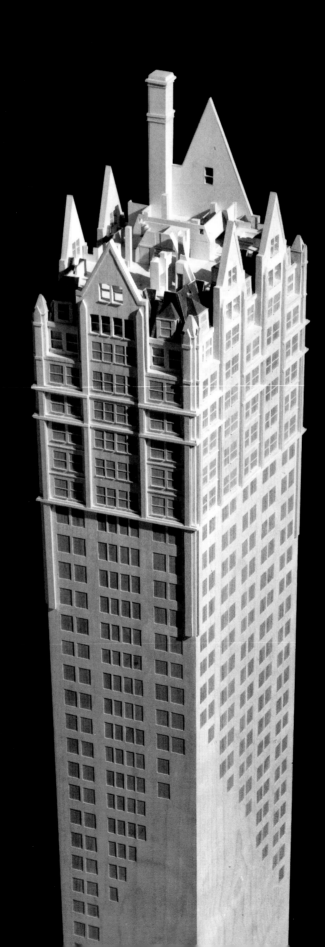

cutaway axonometric

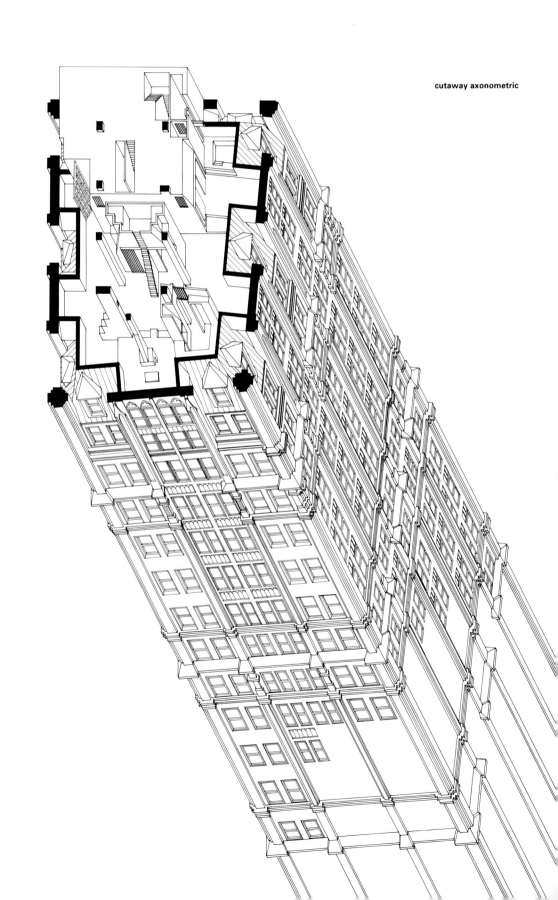

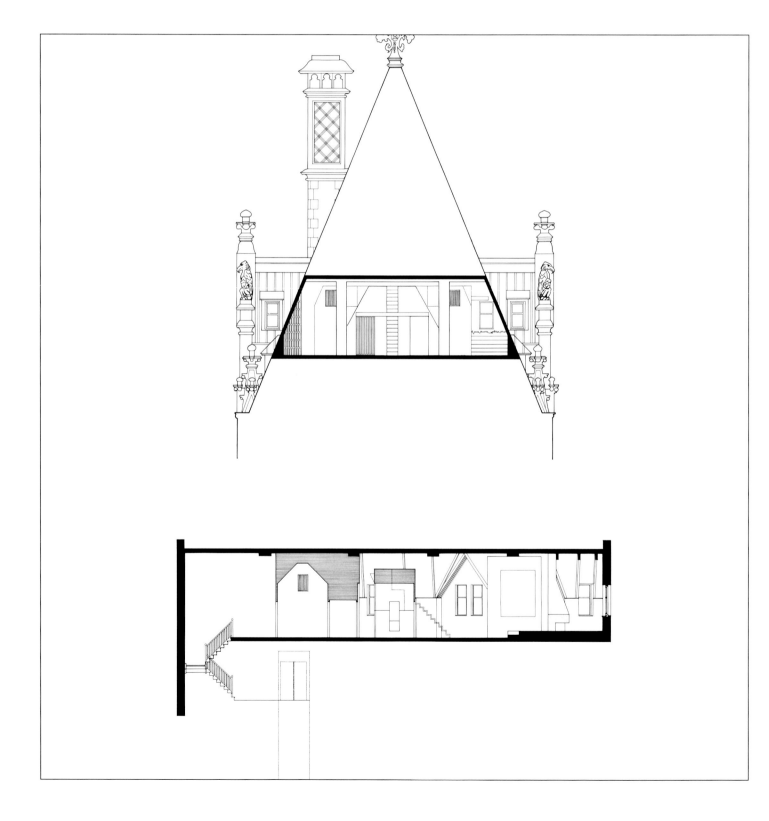

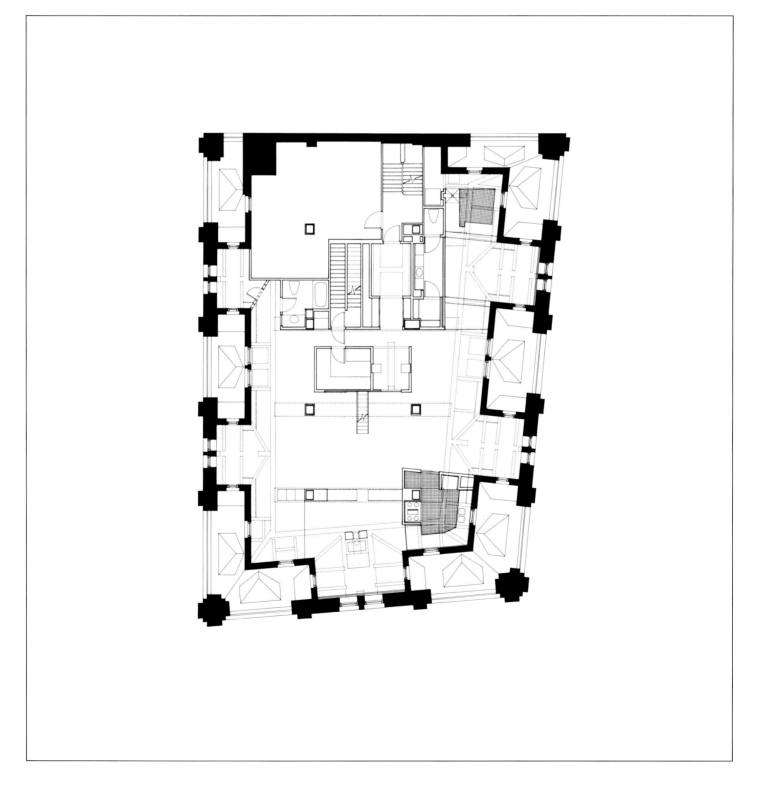

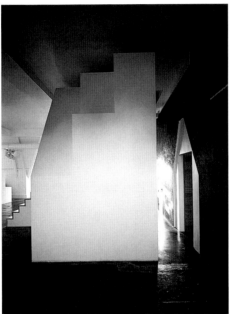

clark ho<u>use</u> ⌐

Hollywood, California   1980

The Clark House pays homage to the Villa Farnese in Caprarola, by Vignola and Michelangelo. I met the Clarks while in Rome, and we visited Caprarola together. Hilary Clark is a Renaissance historian, and Charles an attorney from Chicago. A few years later, when the Clarks decided to relocate to Los Angeles, they asked me to design their new home on a site adjacent to Frank Lloyd Wright's Ennis House in the Hollywood Hills.

The examples set by these great architects

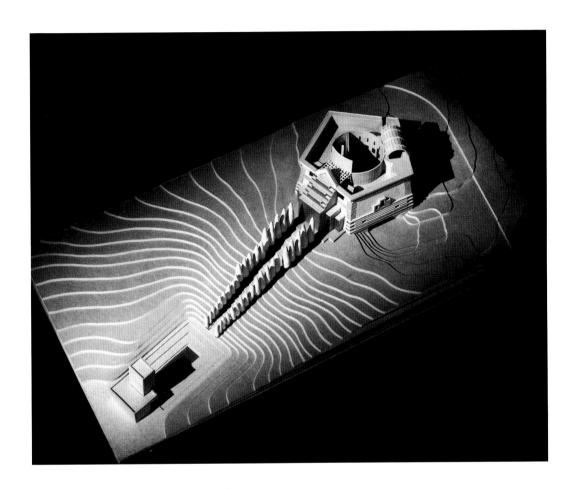

gave us a lot to work with, so we decided from the start to keep the volumetric geometry of the house simple. As the design progressed, a cylinder, then a cube, and finally a pentagon capped the knoll of the site. Centrifugal and faceted, the pentagonal parti gave us the chance to explore the building as a freestanding object and as a series of interrelated facades.

Internal stairs rise on either side of the entrance facade, and living spaces were loaded on three stories around an open cylindrical court. The proportions of the surrounding rooms relate directly to those at the Villa Farnese.

One of the facades frames the entrance to the house, and another opens to a stepped ramp leading to a pool and pool house below. Two of the remaining sides look out over Los Angeles, and the fifth faces the Ennis House. Each of the facades was considered individually, though all follow a pattern of tripartite division and rustication after the Farnese model. By varying the materials at each level and the configuration of openings on each side, a dialogue builds with each facade voicing its own identity but also sounding certain refrains.

In the tradition of Renaissance masonry construction, the corners of the building show a hyperbolic reinforcement of alternating cornerstones. The walls of the pentagon pitch back to an overhanging cornice, first echoing the natural contours of the land, then crowning the rise emphatically.

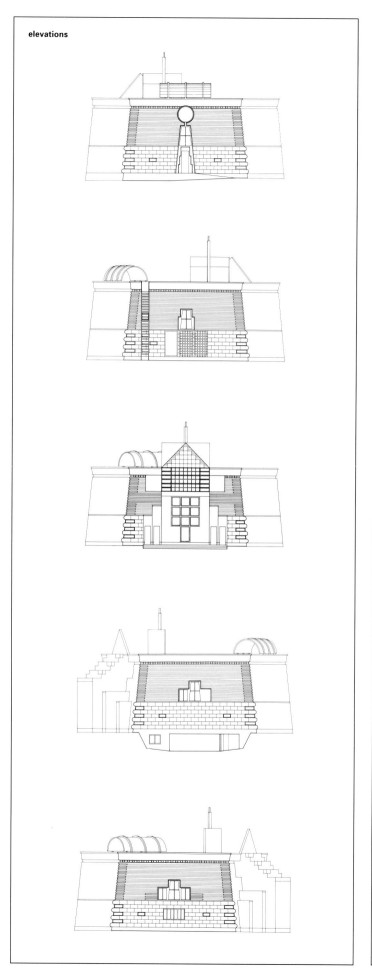

elevations

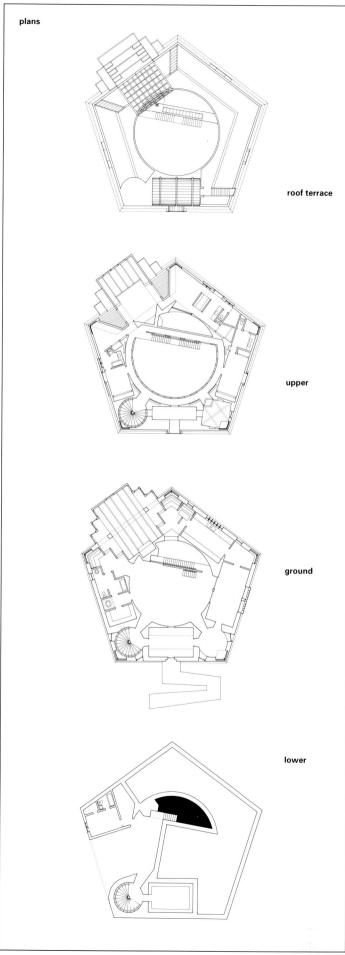

plans

roof terrace

upper

ground

lower

mid-atlantic toyota

Glen Burnie, Maryland   1988

A major renovation of the Mid-Atlantic Toyota headquarters, the commission called for a 41,000-square-foot addition to the existing executive offices designed by Frank Gehry in 1979. Among the first of our office interiors, the Mid-Atlantic Toyota Showroom explores some methods of internal organization that would later govern the designs for Propaganda Films, Bright and Associates, and Virgin Records.

The interiors of the new space were individualized to suit the particular needs and desires of the clients. Differentiation was achieved through a pronounced hierarchy in the overall partition, and through a highly varied palette of shapes and materials. A large skylit atrium contains the double stair which both centers the scheme and leads to the major offices on the second level. Here, as with the "hull" employed at Propaganda Films, we introduced a smaller whole into the larger to give the scheme a nucleus of orientation.

Outside, the building follows the configuration of the property. The facade is made of aluminum panels painted Toyota red. The materials used for the "pods" begin by echoing the Gehry facade and then change as the "pods" themselves transform in size and orientation. As the building tapers, the interior pulls into a long, open arcade connecting the two office cores.

A 300-foot skylit spine also serves as the major gallery for the client's extensive collection of modern art. Other areas throughout the complex serve to encourage a sympathetic interaction between the company employees, the art, and the building itself.

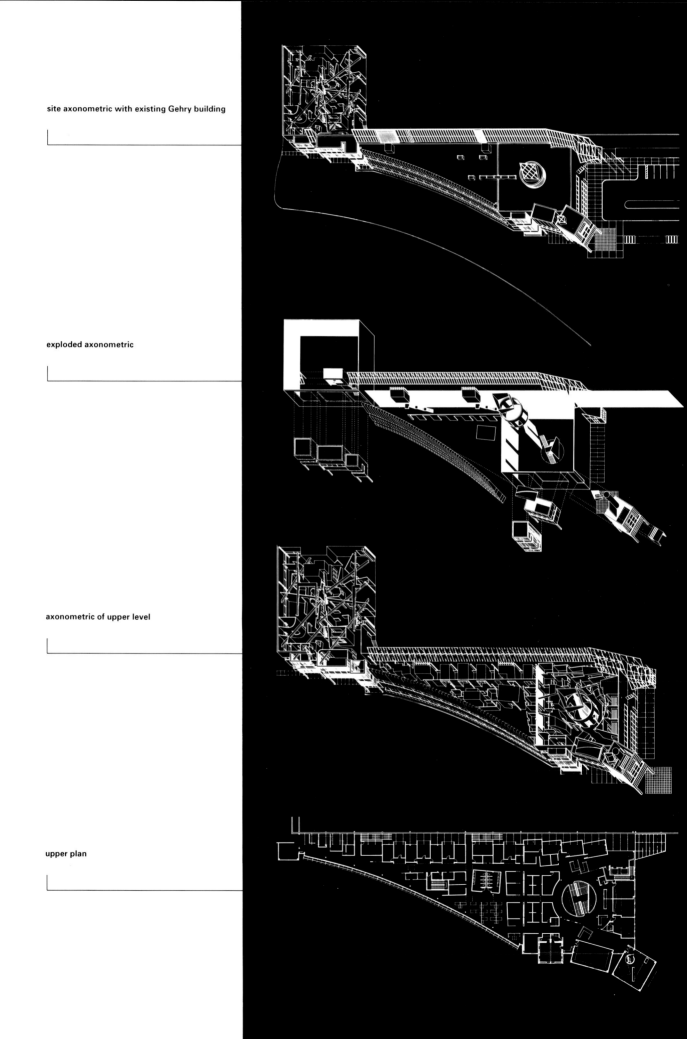

site axonometric with existing Gehry building

exploded axonometric

axonometric of upper level

upper plan

bombyk house

Los Angeles, California   1987

The Bombyk House project, involving an addition and alteration to a hillside home in Hollywood, was never completed. The client, a brilliant filmmaker, died tragically at the age of thirty-four in 1989.

Built in 1922, the original house was known as the first in Los Angeles to use glass block. After purchasing the house, however, Bombyk decided that he did not like glass block and had all of it removed. Then he and his partner, Kip Ohman, asked me to design an addition.

One of the main challenges involved fitting a fairly complicated program into a small, steep site. A strong sense of axiality underpins the program, making this addition and the original a coherent whole. The completed building steps across the contours of the hills, gives way to a set of local axes, and leads the visitor from the rear entry through the larger and more public spaces. The final step in this narrative leads to an open view of the city below.

The clients also had a distinctive collection of furniture and other pieces from the art moderne

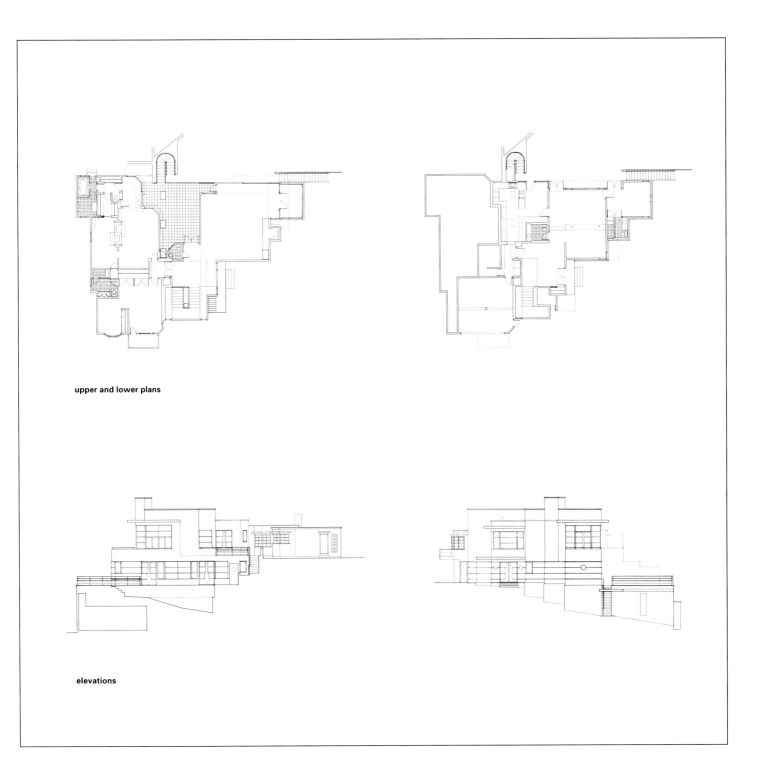

upper and lower plans

elevations

movement. They presented me with a book of the work of Mallet-Stevens, a Parisian modernist active between the First and Second World Wars, stating that his work should serve as a stylistic model for their own home.

We honored their wishes while contending with a series of very real and complex site relationships. One of the solutions to the lack of space on the hill was to position the pool over the garage, not an easy task structurally, but one which mixes two quintessential symbols of California—the automobile and the swimming pool. Porthole windows

from which the swimmer can view the city were installed in the pool. The automobile shuffles in underneath like some miniature submarine moored in the sky.

In the end, we created an interesting essay in synthesis and adaptation. As we searched for ways to bridge the gaps between intention and location, the design came to reflect many of Richard Neutra's attitudes toward siting and detail. As an early advocate of architecture's role in cinema, and vice versa, Mallet-Stevens provided some fresh insight into designing for a producer in the capital of

movie-making. Had the project been realized, it would also have added to the valuable tradition of attempts to create an "indigenous" architecture for Los Angeles.

facing page: *model,* **street view**

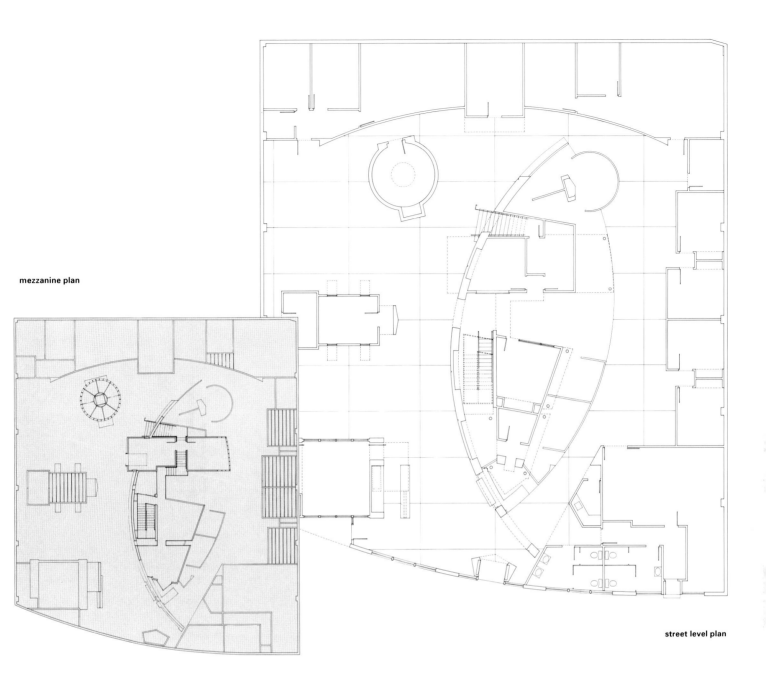

mezzanine plan

street level plan

propaganda fil<u>ms</u> ⏌

Hollywood, California   1988

Rising inside the shell of a classic, bow-string-truss warehouse building on a dusty street in Hollywood are the offices for Propaganda Films.

Work started with the gutting of the warehouse shell. This left a large, dramatic space with heavy, curved trusses, spidery tie-rods, and massive brick and concrete walls. Existing skylights were repaired, and new ones opened up, so that light suffused the building. At the same time, the facade was cleaned, and subtle changes were made to

windows and doors, transforming them from simple barriers between street and building into transition zones and intriguing clues to the new work within.

Several factors shaped the new interior construction. First, the client insisted that the sense of an open warehouse interior not be lost when the new offices were installed. Secondly, as a cooperative creative enterprise, many of the film company staff had a voice in the design and location of various parts of the program. Third, the program was complex, including sound and film editing fa-

cilities, a vault, various meeting rooms for project teams and clients, a range of private offices, screening rooms, lounges, a casting room and other work areas.

At first the client wanted an "office landscape" defined as a series of open partitioned spaces. Because Propaganda was composed of people with distinctly different backgrounds and attitudes, I began to see the organization of the company in terms of an urban village, where serial spatial requirements could ground more "monumental" elements. The original design consists of a vaulted

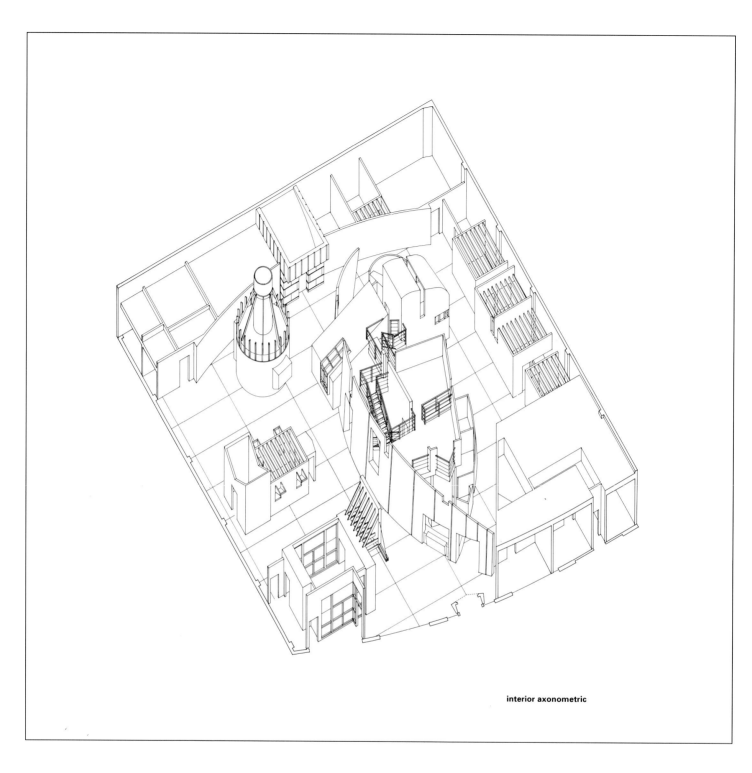

interior axonometric

shell organized by a series of axes, along which the various components are aligned. The bow-string trusses, which restrain the vault, were projected in plan. This image was mirrored and the central office "hull" was made.

The "boat" forms the center of the project, both physically, with its bulk and its vertical and horizontal reach, and analogously, as the location of the offices of the company officers. Besides containing specific rooms, the various pieces create the zones into which the building is divided. And while each piece is formally distinct, the objects also form an overall composition in the building by virtue of their hierarchy of scale, and by their shared colors and materials: drywall painted a soft foam green with exposed redwood-stained wood framing. Refurbished 1940s steel office furniture, discovered by Paul Fortune in a Glendale warehouse, adds a quality of *noir* nostalgia to the otherwise postindustrial work space.

Experiencing Propaganda is akin to working in the film and video business. The space is open, but not open-ended. There is a front desk which serves as the beginning, a large waiting area which serves as the entire residual space, and a somewhat obscured destination—the film vault. Formal relationships reinforce this experience without oppressing it. In effect, the intention was to create a diverse yet coherent village within the shell of the warehouse, a world apart from the industrial zone outside, whose twin inspirations in form and mood were the movie set and a kind of cool, distant, alienation like that found in an Edward Hopper painting —a surrealistic vision of Los Angeles.

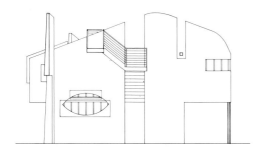

elevations

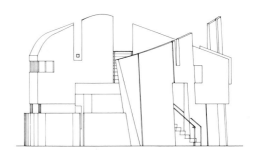

left: plan and section
through video drum

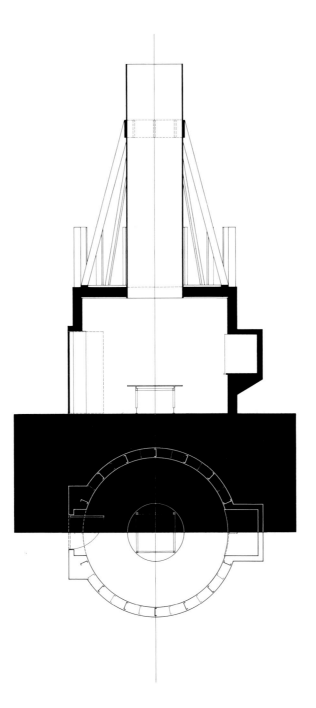

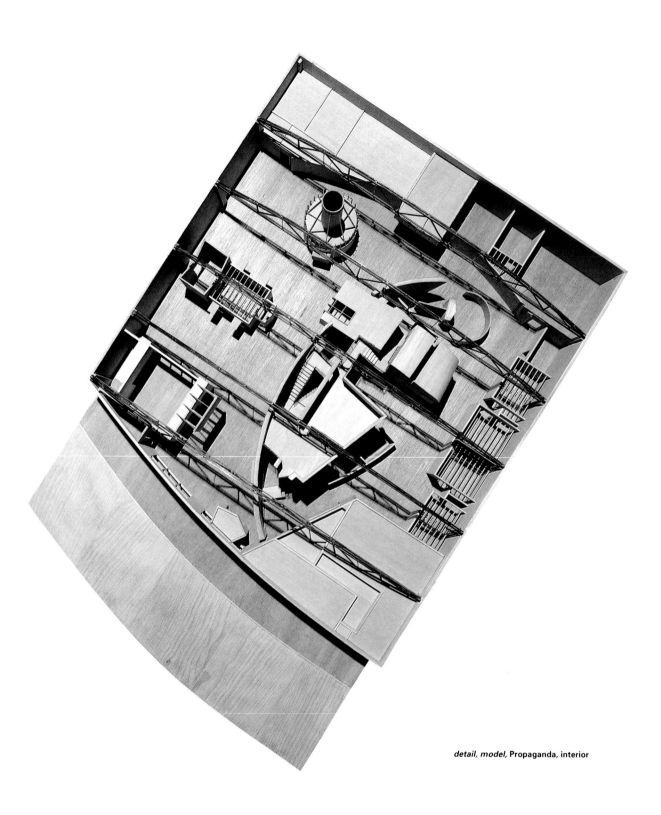

detail, model, Propaganda, interior

altman house

Malibu, California   1988

The Altman House called for the remodeling and interior design of a 2,800-square-foot condominium in Malibu, California. The client approached us with a study model for the renovation that was to heavily influence the final design.

The Altman House was among the first of our many residential projects in California to be bracketed by two concerns: the drama of the locale, and the limitations of town ordinances. One in a long row of beachfront houses in Malibu squeezed be-

tween the Pacific Ocean and the Pacific Coast Highway, the original structure suffered from its poor internal planning. Only the most minute changes to the exterior were permitted under code.

By clearing out most of the existing interior and opening up the oceanside facade as much as possible, the house began to serve the Altmans' needs. The Corbusian emphasis on clear light and clean air became guiding principles for the rearticulation of the interior. Loaded along the streetside wall of the house, the service spaces of the residence buffer the remainder from the highway. The

plan grows more and more open as one moves seaward, as walls become low partitions, baffling but not blocking the western exposure.

Sheltered by an overturned "hull" above, the master bedroom provides a moment's sanctuary from the *plan libre* of the remainder. A skylit stucco-and-steel stairwell anchors the house and recalls Corbusier on two levels. While a gently spiraling handrail plays on Corbu's fixation with snail shells and invertebrate lifeforms, the lightwell itself embodies his tenets for good living—the free circulation of light, air, and human beings.

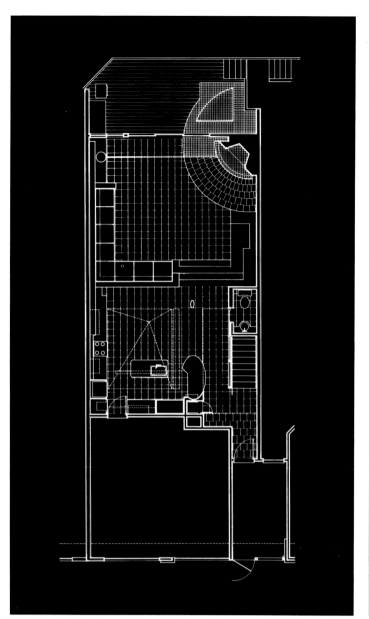

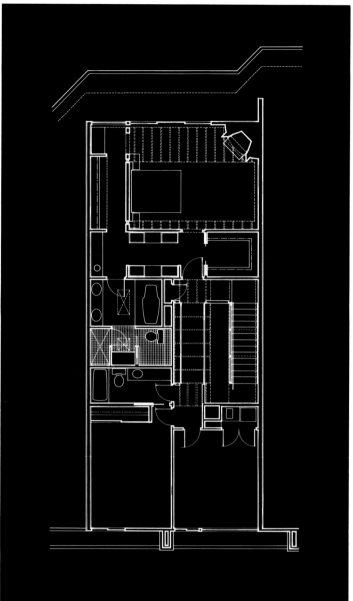

top left and right:
ground and upper plans
left: *model,* sectional veiw

details, model, interior

top left and right:
details, plaster with inset fossils

overleaf: *detail,* Altman fireplace

longitudinal sections

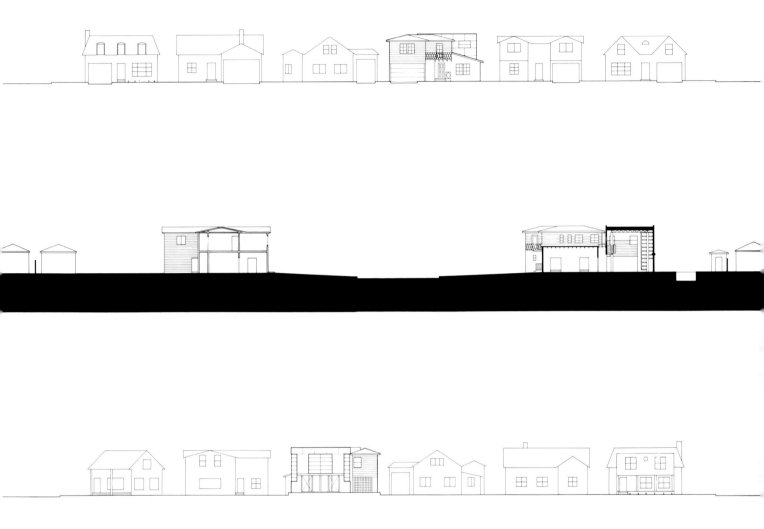

lamy-newton pavilion

Hancock Park, California   1988

In 1988 we completed an addition, remodeling, and landscape design for the Lamy-Newtons. Inserted into the staid community of Hancock Park, the Lamy-Newton Pavilion adds 1,500 square feet of flexible-use space—and much color—to an existing colonial home.

Extremely adventurous clients, the Lamy-Newtons not only favored the new, but asked for the outrageous. A strange inversion of the norm arose in which the architect had to restrain the

clients, and not the opposite. Tempering early schemes that included a faux-Polynesian front elevation, we chose to add a separate structure behind the existing home, so that the new just peeks out from behind the old.

The pavilion is divorced from the main house in almost all respects. Fitted into the "L" of the original, the addition obeys strict principles of symmetry and balance that oppose the discreet suburban asymmetry of the original. Almost cubic, the pavilion is unbroken in plan and open in section to a double-story height. A gallery/balcony provides a com-

plete view of the studio, and a mock-ceremonial perch from which to address the "assembled."

A palette of deep primary colors—maroon, mustard, navy—sets off the stark black and white of the existing home, and questions the odd abstraction and humility of most residential hues. Following the scalar divide between the two structures, the windows and sliding double doors of the pavilion invent idioms of their own by mixing the motifs of Rudolph Schindler and commonplace industrial forms.

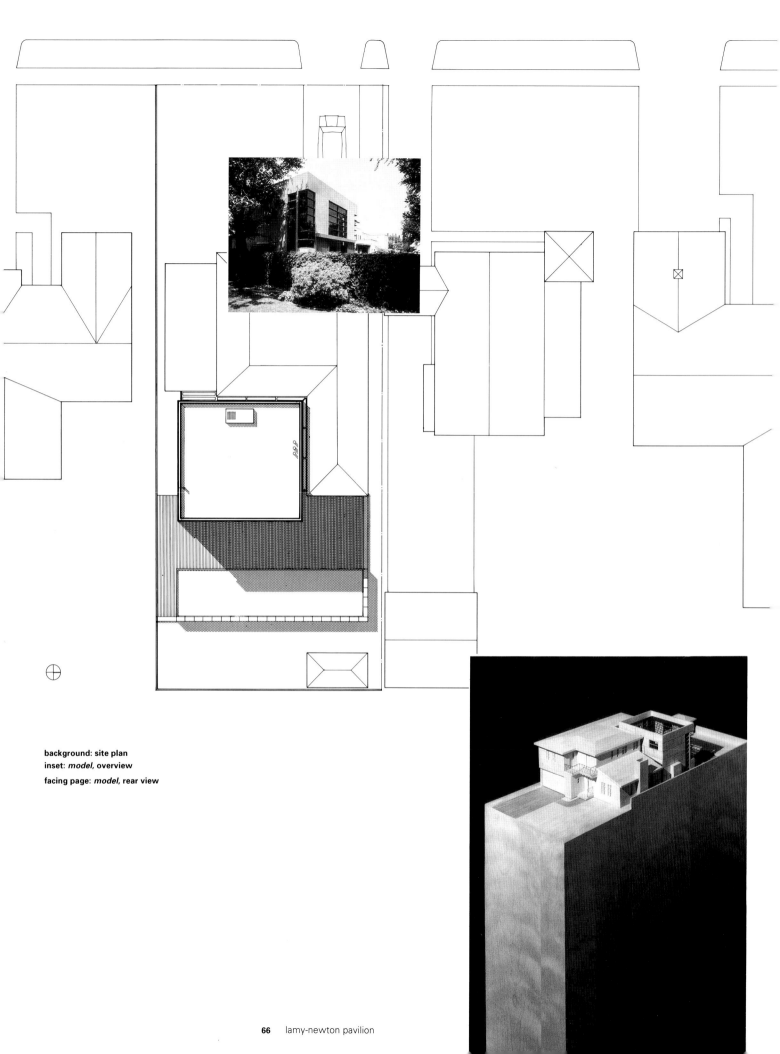

background: site plan
inset: *model*, overview
facing page: *model*, rear view

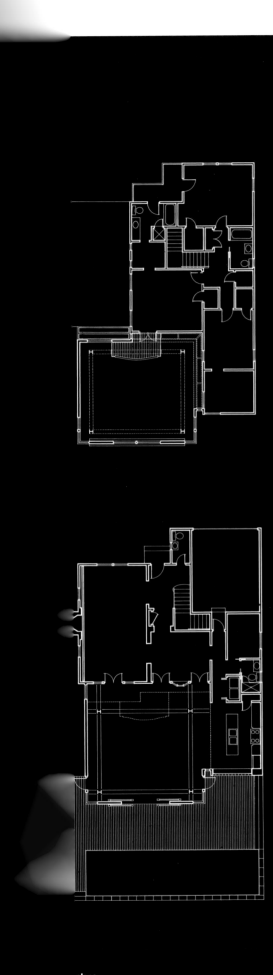

plans

detail, balcony

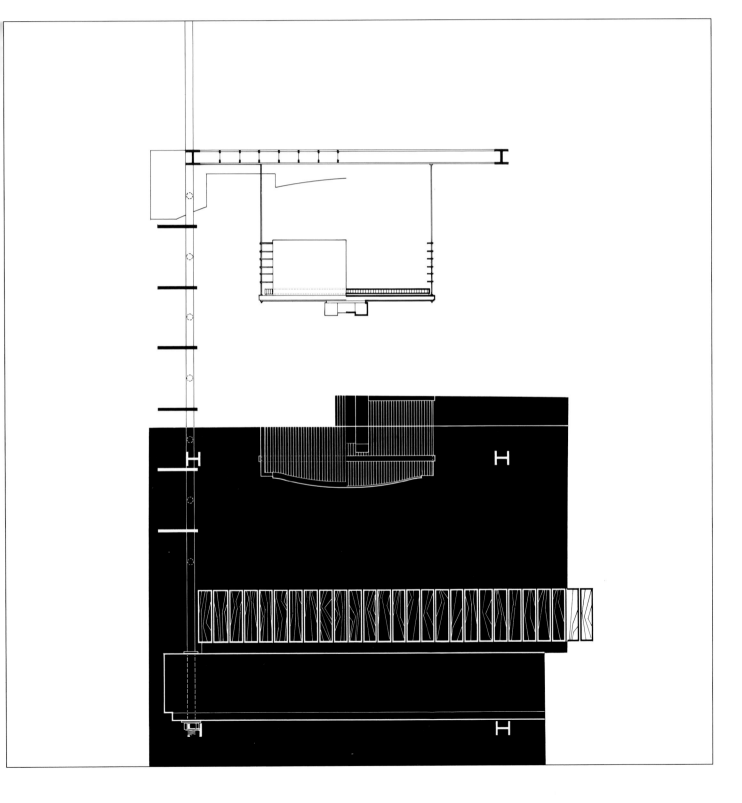

architecture tomorrow, a walker art center exhibit

Minneapolis, Minnesota
October 1988–January 1989

The first of five architectural installations at the Walker Art Center in Minneapolis, "Architecture Tomorrow" set the tone for the series. "Both art and settings for art," the pavilions of the Walker exhibit embodied many of my concerns as an architect, while also displaying our work in a clear and accessible manner.

The show consisted of six minimal wooden pieces—pavilions— arranged in a room, each a sin-

gular place for the display of our work. The display panels were made of a material resembling concrete called glaswal, and they were hooked onto the wooden frames by a series of steel clips. In essence, the wooden pavilions became scaffolding on which to hang ideas. Each one represented a different form of structure and architectural pattern; they announced a vitality of construction and a potential for different forms. They became a framework on which to display fragments of an industrial and mass-media vernacular which, in turn, stands against the abstract backdrop of the sea,

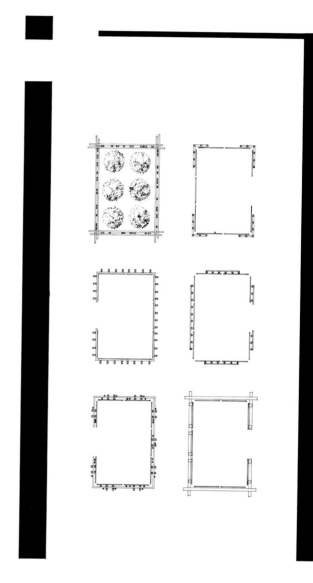

gallery plan with installation

desert, mountains, and freeways of LA. I used this technique of montage, collage, and broken narrative to emphasize a whole range of stylistic diversity, with hopes of retaining a different theme in each pavilion. I also wanted to express a sensual handling of materials as well as a certain sense of theatricality. Lastly, I wanted to visualize the themes of refuge and the need to escape.

Five of the six pavilions allowed the viewer to enter and surround himself with the installation. The sixth, however, did not. It consisted of six live pine trees placed within the protection of one of the pavilions; the viewer could touch the trees only through the wooden slats. Here, I wished to express the idea of refuge. The trees were contained in a "safe oasis" which the spectator was prevented from fully entering by the wooden grid. The viewer was kept at a distance; he could perceive the idealized world of trees but was prevented from fully being a part of it.

The Walker show was, in turn, documented and elaborated by Kamal Kozah in his video production "Architecture Tomorrow: The Architecture of Frank Israel." In the video we were able to introduce narrative overlays and graphic "refractions" of the original images that transform the film into a hypnotic meditation on the act of design.

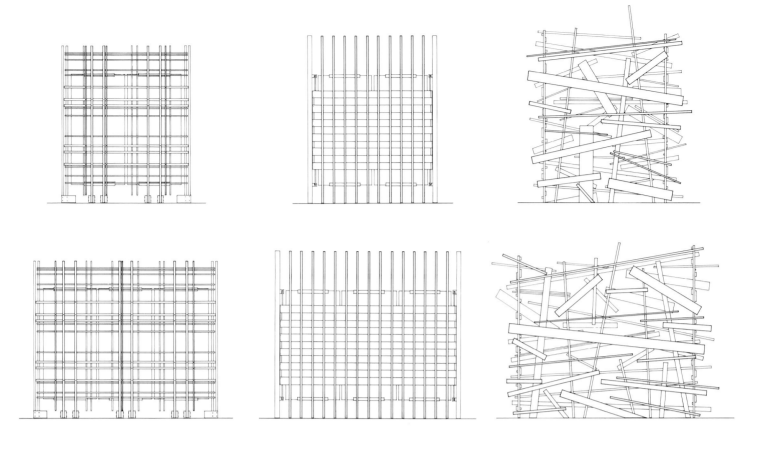

pavilion elevations

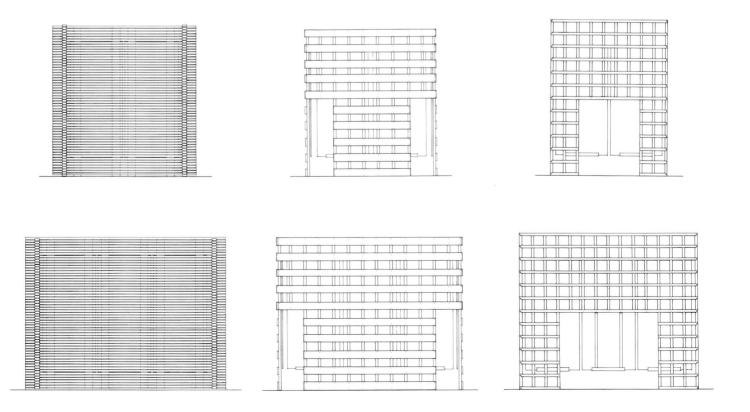

arango-berry house

Beverly Hills, California   1989

The Arango-Berry project involved a remodeling and an addition to an existing residence for a screenwriter and producer. The original 1950s structure was completely gutted, the exterior scraped away, and new elevations designed.

The overall composition is unified by a large overlaying roof rebuilt to enclose the heating, air conditioning, and ventilation ducts. The roof is covered in bonderized sheet metal. This material is also used on the addition, which contains the mas-

ter bathroom and dressing area.

The interiors were stripped down to their original 1950s frame. Views of the city were opened up by using very large picture windows and walls of transparent glass block. The cabinetry is pulled away from the original armature and updated. Stereo and television cabinets, the master bedroom fireplace, and the bed itself were built in fingrade plywood with sandblasted steel details and stacked glass. The entrance gallery is capped by an undulating soffit in plaster with recessed lighting.

The gallery leads into the house from the large

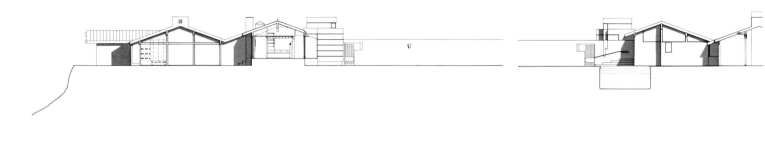

top: longitudinal sections
below: *sketch*, sectional study

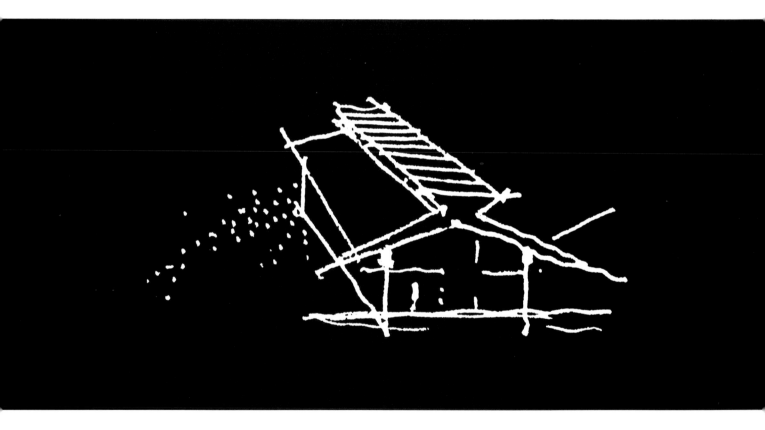

pivoting front door with its steel and glass lintel.

The pool was left untouched, and the brick deck around it extended to the new concrete steps and blue stucco garden wall. This wall is a major compositional element of the house; it links the garage to the front door, and is then brought inside, following the entry gallery to the main living space.

The influences here are twofold. Contemporary influences are manifested in the juxtapositions of materials and styles in the street and ridge elevations. Historically, the materials and the volumetric relationships of various forms are intended to recall

Schindler and Neutra.

A second addition is currently being planned, and it is intended to recall the work of John Lautner in its sculptural frenzy. A serrated tower wedged into the southeast edge of the site will recompose all the bedrooms and extend out from the home in a series of cantilevered decks.

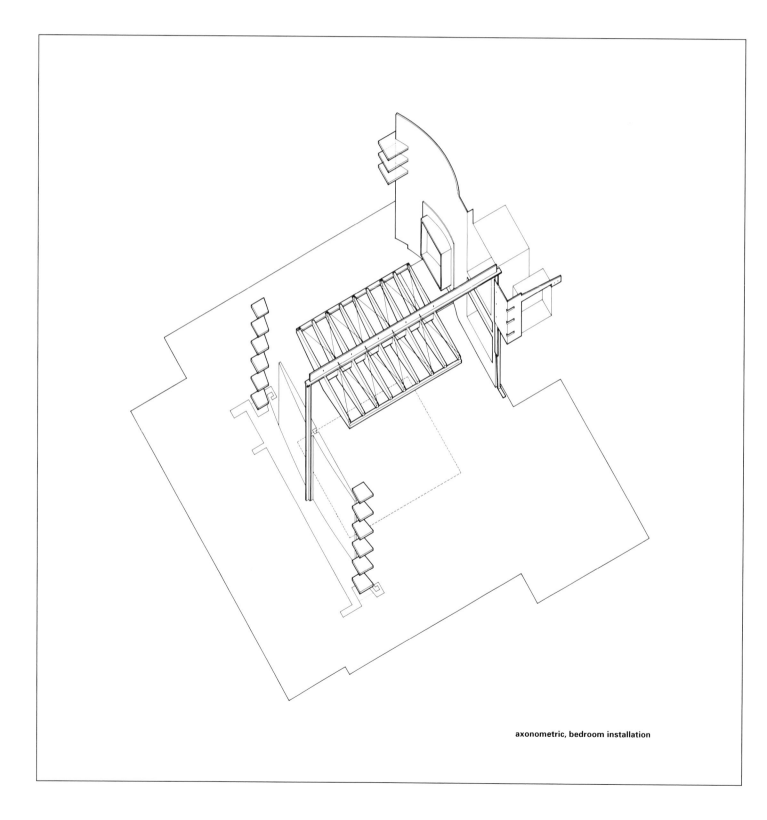

axonometric, bedroom installation

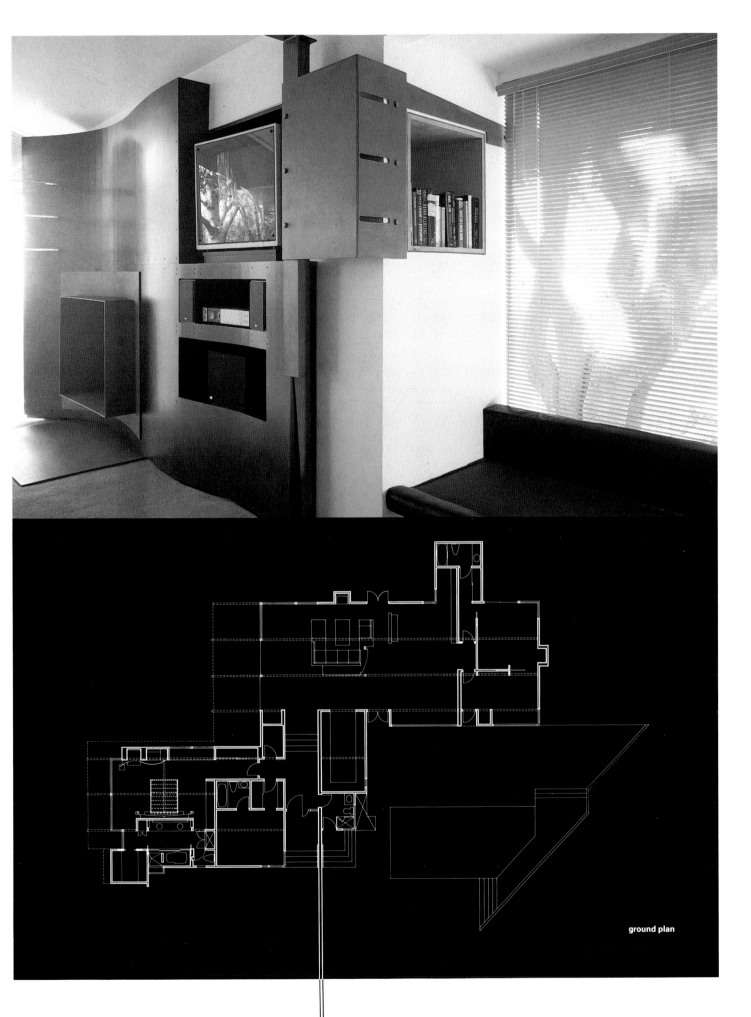

ground plan

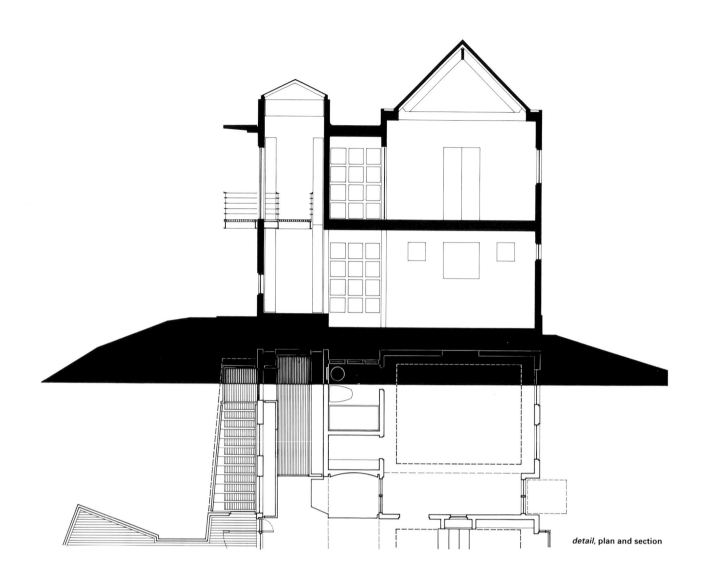

detail, **plan and section**

randy and dianne roberts house |

Hollywood, California   1989

The Roberts House, in the hills above Lake Holly-wood Reservoir, expands on an existing 1950s ranch house. The remodeled original and the addition were designed as an assemblage of distinct parts that lock together. Each component is distinguished on the exterior, and the interior is comprised of a series of rooms that segue from one to the next. The addition culminates in a promontory with views towards the San Fernando valley and the Hollywood Hills.

The design reordered the existing house by imposing a system of axial corridors and circulation paths. The main axis runs from a tower bridge to the kitchen, giving the house its "spine." The length of this corridor is then modulated by a number of transverse axes and spatial oppositions that follow from the outside to the inside and then outside again. In elevation, the existing windows and openings are blown up to a scale befitting the tower. As the new axis orients the overall plan, the tower pins the entire composition to the ground plane.

At street level, two studios provide work places for the couple. Above the studios are two bed-rooms for the children, each roofed separately and linked by a small library that emerges into the street facade. The stair joining both levels floats in a double-story space lit from above by skylights. An open-grate bridge ties the addition to the public areas of the older house. A large, open-plan kitchen—the focus of the home, and where the Roberts spend most of their time together—terminates the axis begun by the bridge.

hard rock hotel

Las Vegas, Nevada 1987

Planned for a site just off the strip, the Hard Rock Hotel came into the office with much of the design completed. The facade of the hotel would stay, we were told, but would be customized in the tradition of the Hard Rock Cafes. With cherried-out vintage Cadillacs jutting out over their entrance, and rock and roll instruments plastering their interiors, the Hard Rock Cafes gave us a lot of imagery to work with. In addition to the revamped exterior, two restaurant interiors were called for, one a 24-hour cafe the other a gourmet Morton's of Las Vegas.

A new entrance defies the rigid and vaguely classical detailing of the existing design. Set at a rakish angle, a vast neon-lit piano keyboard plays over head as one enters the hotel. Though Pop in its tactics, the keyboard is scaled and detailed to read more as a graceful louvred entrance piece than as Oldenberg icon. Unlike signage that would seek to veil its structure, the systems of support are here meant to draw as much attention as the grand gesture itself. A single heavy pier lifts one side of the keyboard, while a space-frame truss secures the remainder and frames the entrance proper.

Though hardly understated, the new entrance sequence boasts a certain subtlety next to, or below, the *coup de grace* of the customization. High in the Las Vegas skyline, a Stratocaster of epic proportions thrusts out into the desert air. The gargantuan guitar arose out of the client's concern for visibility from the strip, and the realization that at this scale, no Cadillac was going to cut it.

facing page:
model, entry canopy

top to bottom:
elevations, entrance
plans, rendering

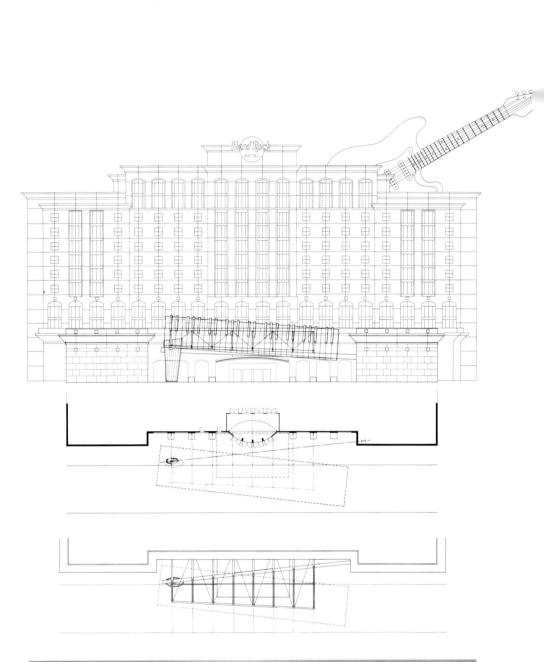

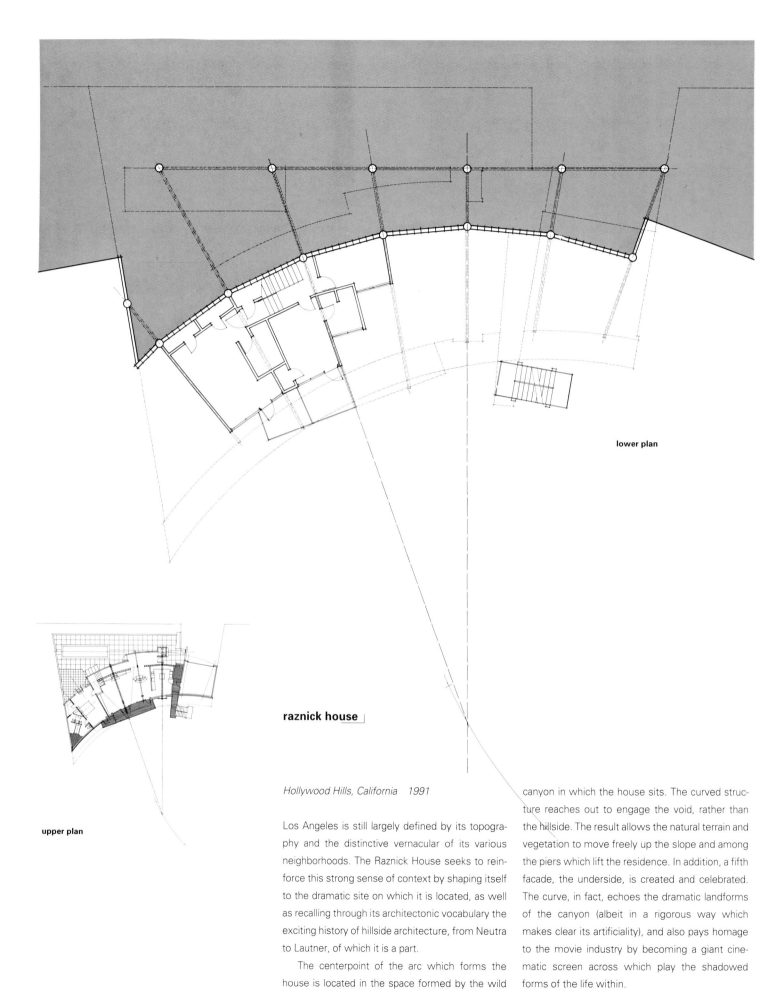

lower plan

raznick ho<u>use</u> ⌐

upper plan

Hollywood Hills, California   1991

Los Angeles is still largely defined by its topography and the distinctive vernacular of its various neighborhoods. The Raznick House seeks to reinforce this strong sense of context by shaping itself to the dramatic site on which it is located, as well as recalling through its architectonic vocabulary the exciting history of hillside architecture, from Neutra to Lautner, of which it is a part.

The centerpoint of the arc which forms the house is located in the space formed by the wild canyon in which the house sits. The curved structure reaches out to engage the void, rather than the hillside. The result allows the natural terrain and vegetation to move freely up the slope and among the piers which lift the residence. In addition, a fifth facade, the underside, is created and celebrated. The curve, in fact, echoes the dramatic landforms of the canyon (albeit in a rigorous way which makes clear its artificiality), and also pays homage to the movie industry by becoming a giant cinematic screen across which play the shadowed forms of the life within.

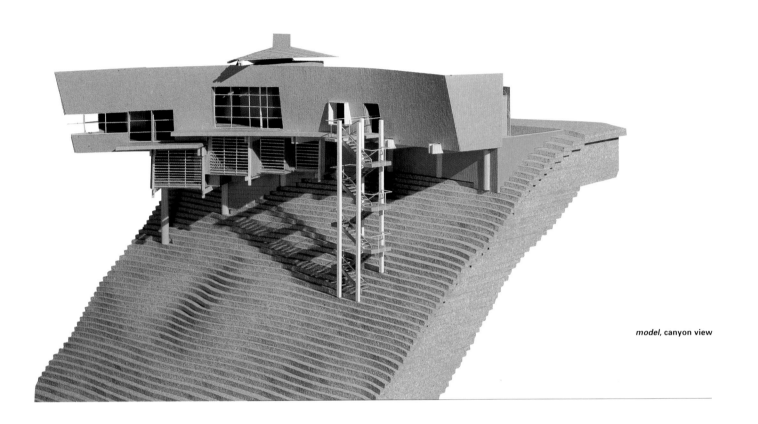

model, canyon view

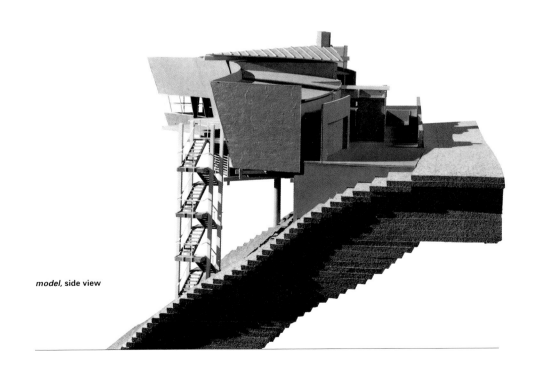

model, side view

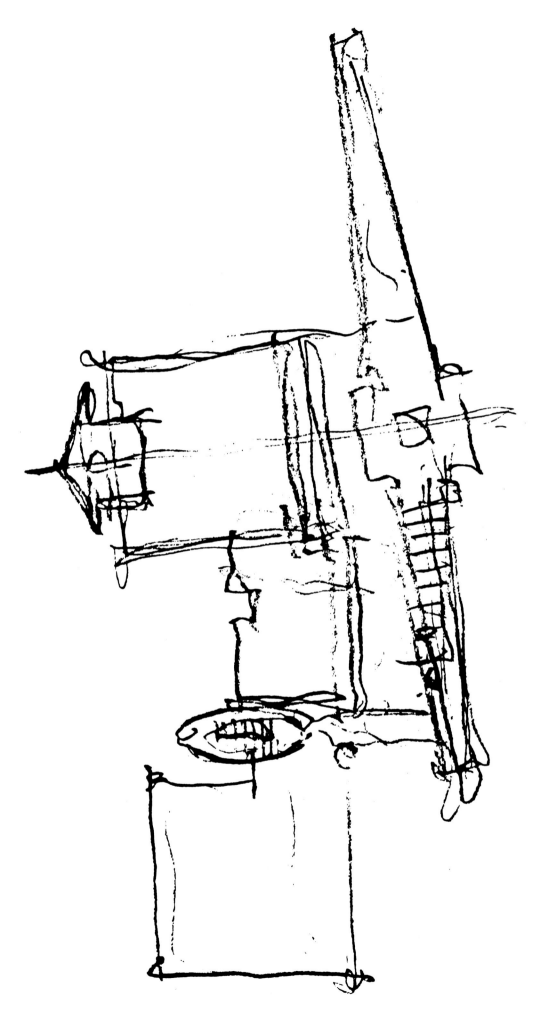

sketch, schematic plan

facing page:
lower right: site plan

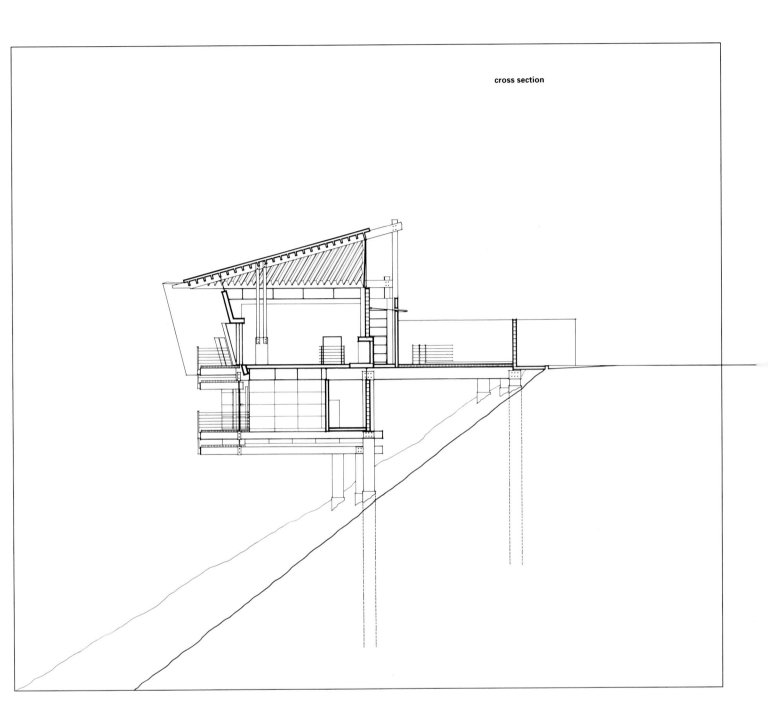

Along the street, the concave form of the house creates a plaza between the street wall so common in the Hollywood Hills, and the curved building. Upon entering this space, the visitor encounters a cistern waterfall—a traditional gesture of greeting in arid Los Angeles—immediately adjacent to the front door and aligned in composition with the requisite swimming pool.

The curve is not dominant in all realms: the roofscape is fragmented into separate forms over the living room, dining room, and master bath. A guest apartment sits above the garage, entered via the stair tower. This tower, the major vertical feature in the design, also visually anchors the building to the hillside.

The row of concrete piles which literally hold the site together are continued up to become the basic structure for the house. Glu-lam beams span between. The curved elevations are screens of troweled plaster and glass; the roofs are metal; and the guest bedrooms which hang below the curve are constructed of wood frame, glass, and steel. Inside the building, a field of curved walls parallels the direction of movement lengthwise through the house. Perpendicular to these, elements of structure, the fireplace, and the roof forms all group around cross axes to develop distinct places within the continuum of space.

bright and associates ⌐

Venice, California   1991

The project at 901 W. Washington Boulevard in Venice involved the renovation and transformation of three existing buildings into the design offices for Keith Bright and Associates. This group of buildings, dating from 1929, served originally as a train shed, then a funeral parlor, and most recently as the offices of Charles and Ray Eames. The Eameses first occupied the premises as their workspace in 1943.

The two larger brick buildings, previously connected by a small fire door, are now physically linked by a sheet-metal "tunnel." This tunnel is a major link in the entry sequence and disguises the transition from one building to the other. A two-story skylit atrium sits at the entry to the tunnel, surrounded by administrative facilities. This space is a parallelogram in plan, derived from the irregular angles of the existing buildings. Outside, a steel-and-glass canopy defines the commencement of the dramatic entry sequence.

At the opposite end of the "tunnel," in the largest and oldest building on the site, lies an open multipurpose space dominated by an inverted cone sheathed in plywood which contains a large conference room. Flanking this area are the executive offices. From this point adjacent facilities are arranged along a major longitudinal path which extends from this space to the east. One moves along this interior "street" past the executive design offices, into the large design room, and on into the production area. This axis is terminated by an obelisk demarcating the photo reproduction area, which is lighted from above.

Outside, various sculptural objects have been

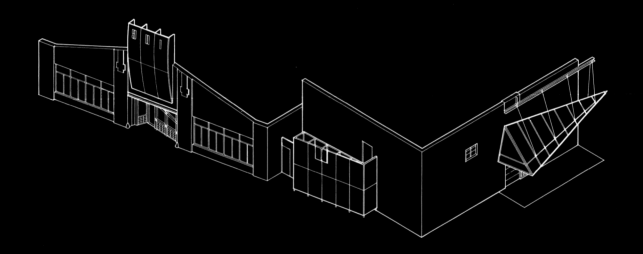

facing page: isometric elevation

top: ground plan with
cross sections
lower right: *detail,* axonometric,
office installation

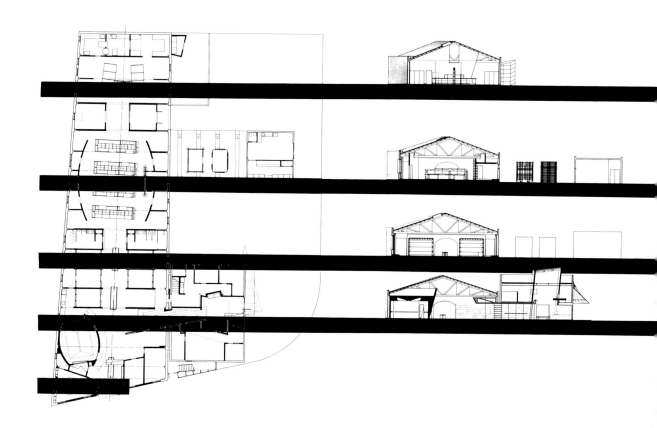

placed strategically on the existing structures. These serve to link the group of buildings to its Venice context, as well as mark the location of the entrance, the fire stair, and the numerical building sign. These are constructed of steel, glass, and sheet metal. The interior atrium is visible as it pops up above the roof. The history of the site determined a strategy in which much of the exterior was unchanged. When Charles Eames decided to paint portions of the exterior white, his decision was based on a belief that the reflections of the surrounding trees, telephone poles, and airplanes in the sky above were tantalizing moving portraits, appropriate visual statements of urban life. Our exterior attempts to update the Eameses' vision while providing Bright and Associates with a place they can call their own.

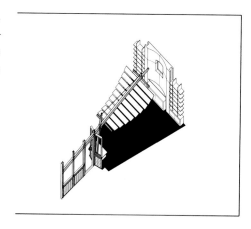

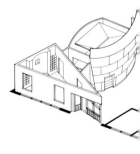

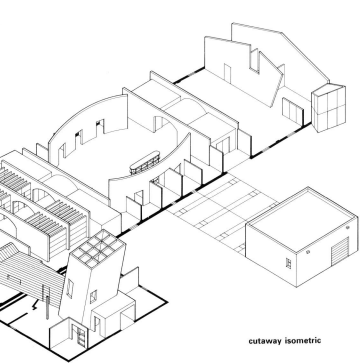

cutaway isometric

art pavilion |

Beverly Hills, California   1991

The project is a freestanding pavilion situated next to a large hillside home in Los Angeles. The pavilion contains a gallery for the large art collection of the client, and two floors of studio and related spaces.

The art pavilion is located in an exclusive residential neighborhood, on a six-acre site which pitches down to a stream and a dense eucalyptus grove. The building is intended both to complement the prevailing Mediterranean style of the homes in the area and to move beyond them. It

seeks to appear as a great ark, containing an important collection of abstract expressionist art, yet empowered by its contents to become a piece of art in the terraced sculpture garden. At the same time, through its grand stairs, terraces, and an outdoor loggia, the pavilion actively engages the site. Large corner windows also serve to bring in views of trees and sky, while bowing to the tradition started in Los Angeles by Wright and Schindler of the mitered glass corner and the exploded box. These windows also prescribe rhythmic breaks in the interior where art cannot be hung.

The top floor of the pavilion is a gallery with a twenty-eight-foot ceiling carried on large timber trusses. Movable walls allow the room to become a reception or lecture space while regulating natural light. The architectural focus of the space is a floating stair linking the upper main gallery with a lower gallery, outdoor loggia, and dining area. The two-story base also contains a small photography gallery, archive, guest quarters, and conservation lab. An underground passage connects this area to the main house.

The upper wall exteriors are clad with fiberglass

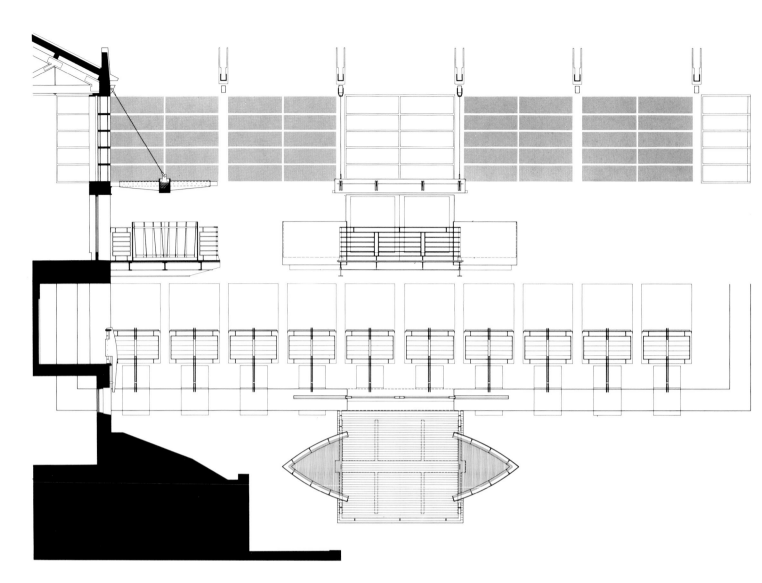

facing page:
top: garden view, composite plan,
section, elevation
bottom: *model*, garden view

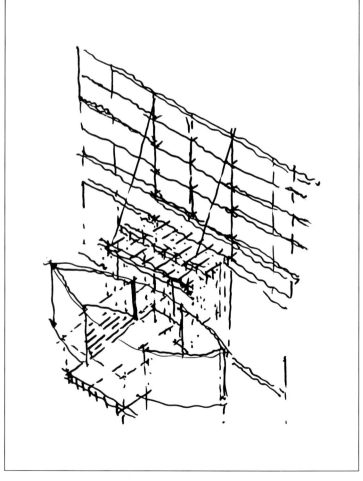

reinforced concrete and glass panels set in ma-
hogany frames. The lower walls are stucco to
match the existing house. The roof is sheet metal
and custom tile, with elaborated scuppers.

A giant boat-shaped balcony hangs over the
garden side of the building. Constructed of steel
and wood, it will be covered with wisteria and
bougainvillea. A smaller version of the great ark, it
is intended to appear as if it were being raised from
the garden below.

model, **cross section**

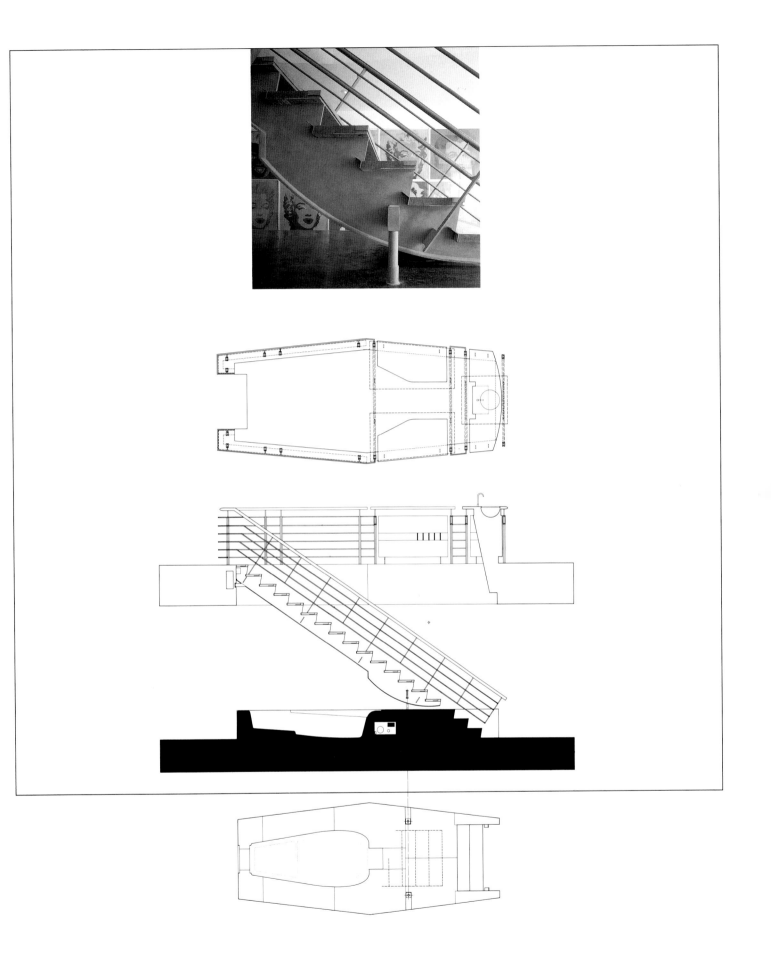

detail, gallery stair, plan and section

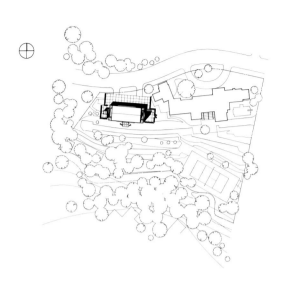

above: site plan   below: loggia level plan   facing page: gallery level plan

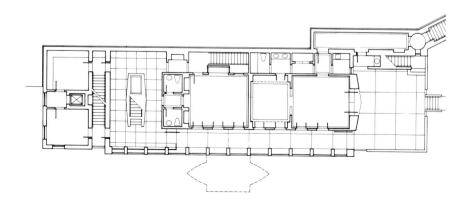

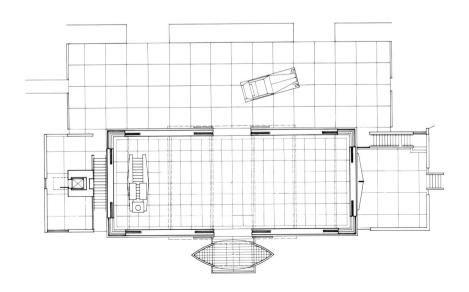

top inset: Virgin I, site model
with Gehry's Chiat building
below: Virgin I, ground plan

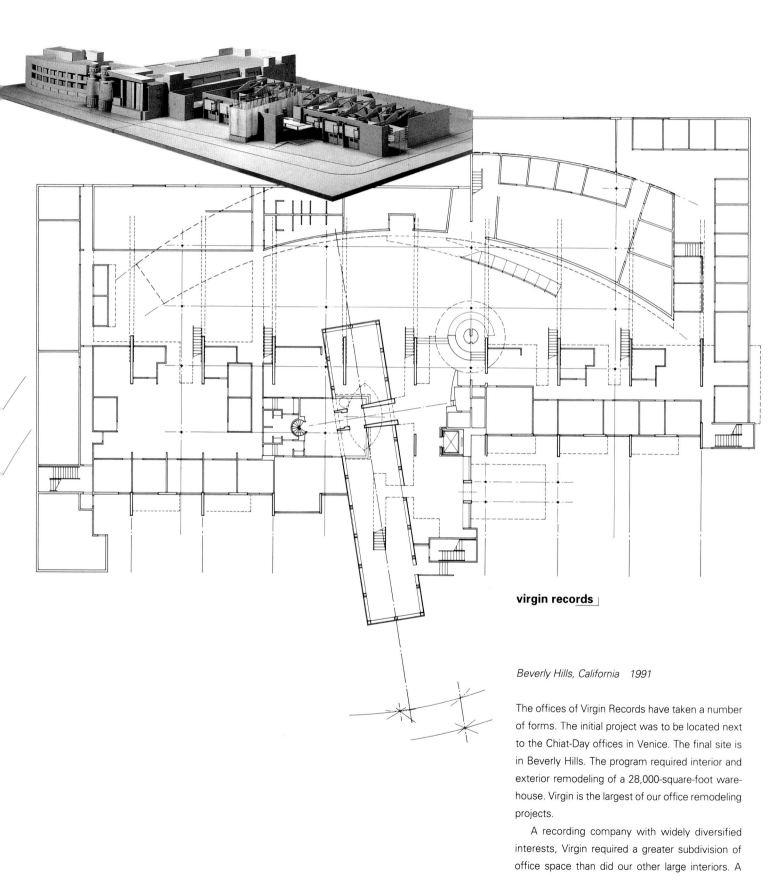

virgin records |

Beverly Hills, California   1991

The offices of Virgin Records have taken a number
of forms. The initial project was to be located next
to the Chiat-Day offices in Venice. The final site is
in Beverly Hills. The program required interior and
exterior remodeling of a 28,000-square-foot warehouse. Virgin is the largest of our office remodeling
projects.

A recording company with widely diversified
interests, Virgin required a greater subdivision of
office space than did our other large interiors. A

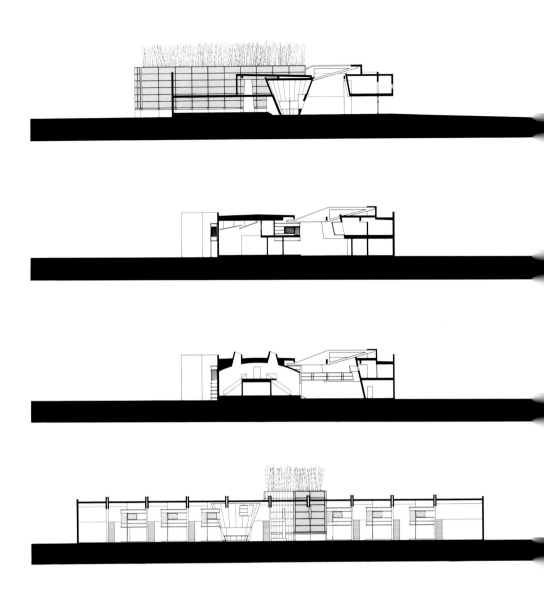

Virgin I sections

corporate division between the business and creative offices led to a near-symmetrical split in the plan of the interior. In this scheme we opted for a tighter axial development than at Bright and Associates or Propaganda Films. We lined most of the paths with private offices. The grid of closed spaces came to serve as a datum defining the "negative" space of a T-shaped pathway.

At the intersection of the "T," a solid cylindrical amphitheater presents a third zone of space within the interior. As the paths were carved from the office grid, the stairs and stepped seating of the am-phitheater were conceived in the same manner of reductive sculpting. They appear cut from a solid round of material, incised alternately for seating and movement.

Following the earlier designs for the Venice site (described in the "Cities Within" essay), the exterior plays subtly on the name and nature of Virgin. A low "V" marks the entrance to the headquarters, and a long curving outer wall presses out toward the street. The billowing curve recalls the "hulls" in our previous work and coyly suggests that Virgin may be more "pregnant" with inspiration than its name would indicate. Though no longer affronted by the multivalent architectural machismo of the site on Main Street in Venice, the Virgin complex in Beverly Hills fends off the cool advances of her neighbors with graceful composure.

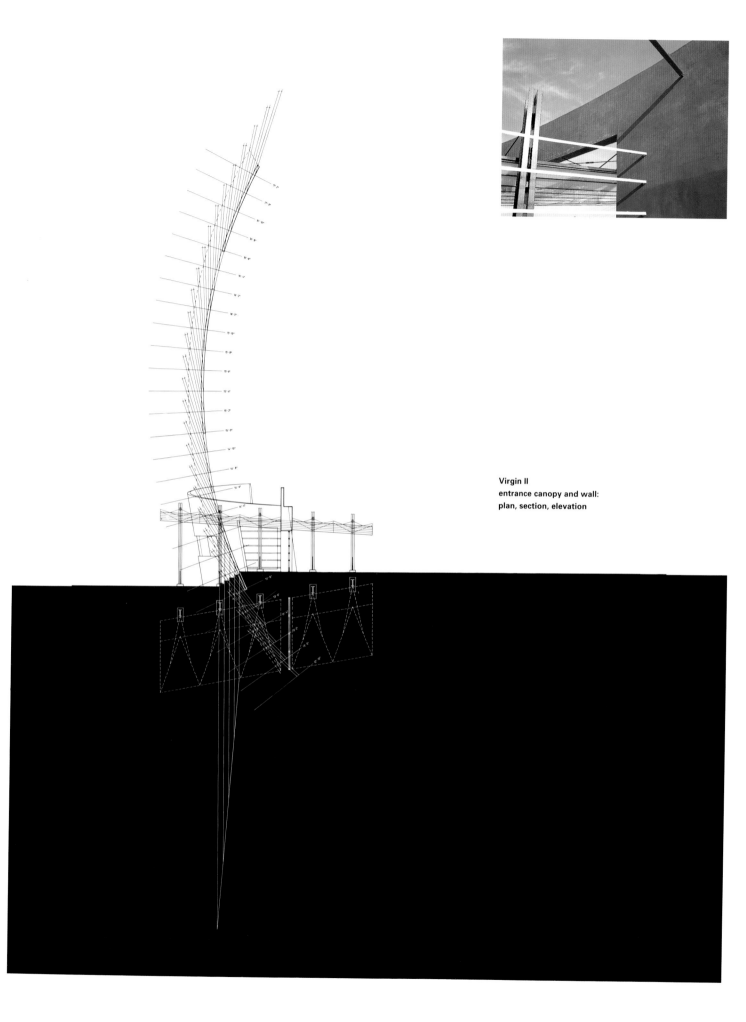

Virgin II
entrance canopy and wall:
plan, section, elevation

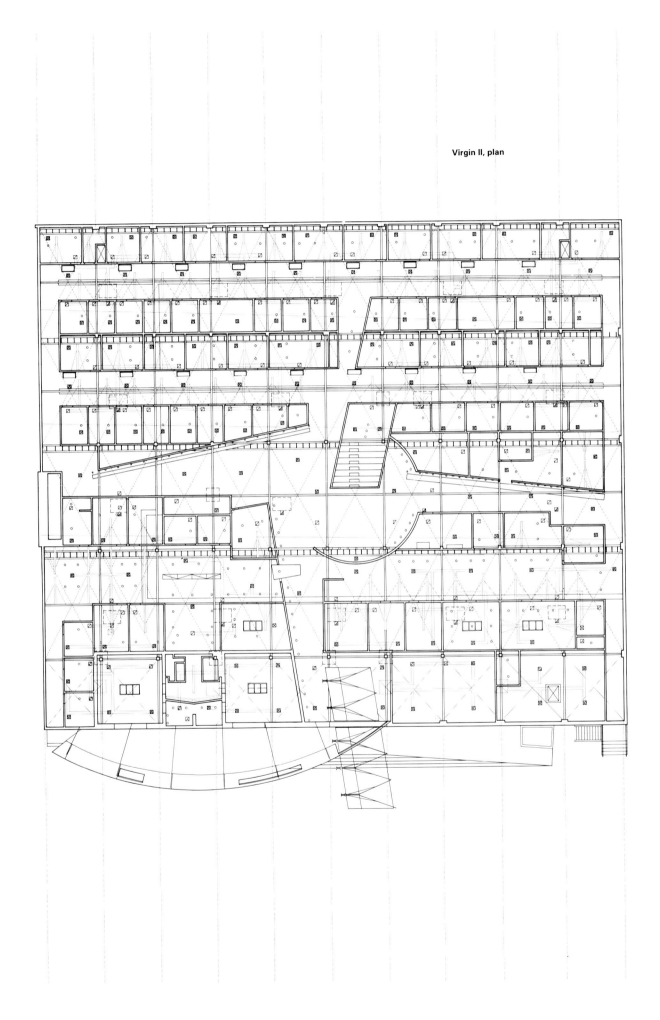

Virgin II, plan

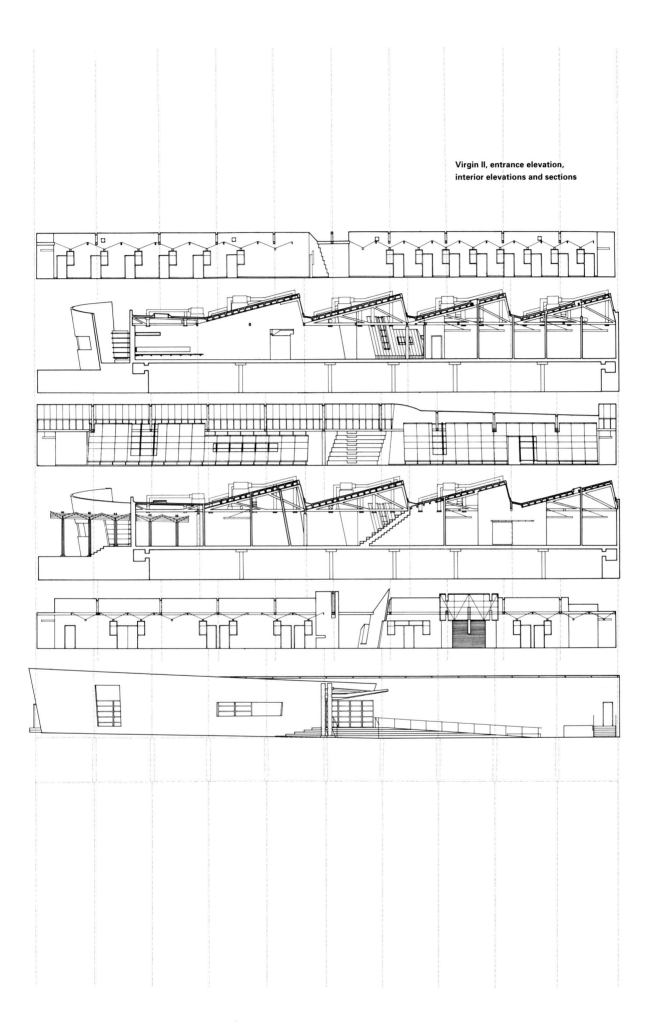

Virgin II, entrance elevation,
interior elevations and sections

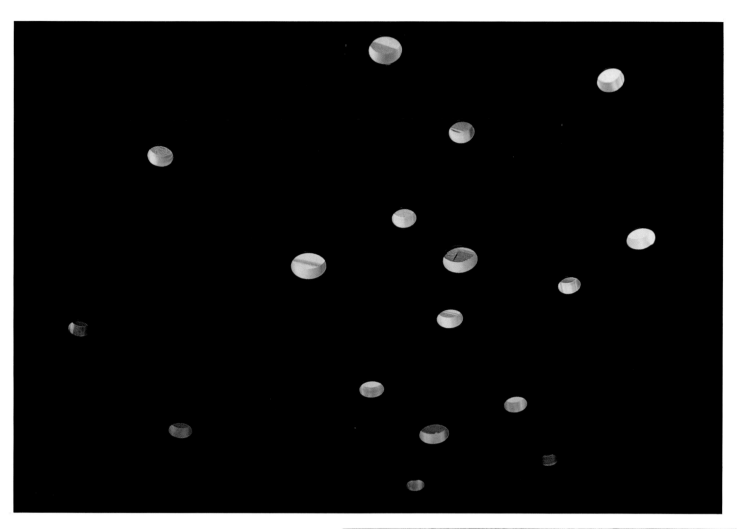

facing page: door hardware

above: pin light
right: *detail,* reception area

goldberg-bean house

Hollywood, California   1991

The Goldberg-Bean project, an addition to a 1950s
ranch-style house in the Hollywood Hills, will more
than double the size of the existing building.

The residence, located on a small hillside street
in a quiet residential neighborhood, is surrounded
by homes which run the entire span of regional
styles, from Spanish revival to postmodern. The
existing house sits on a curved, gently sloping site
that is graced with a magnificent series of oak
trees and a spectacular view. The clients asked

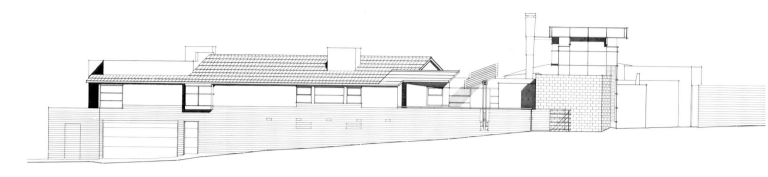

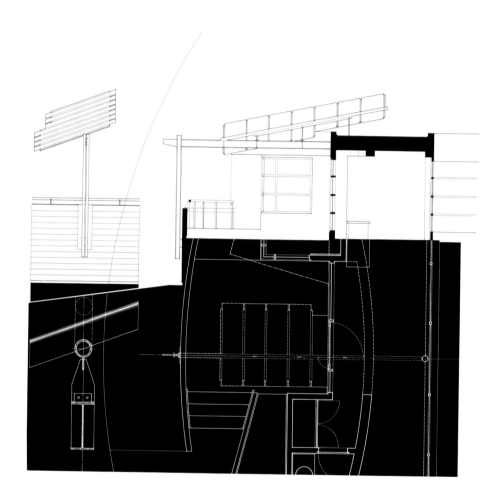

the architect to remodel the existing house, while adding a private realm that completely transforms the site, projecting a series of dramatically articulated, three-dimensional volumes beyond the original house and into the garden. Another small bedroom is planned for the opposite end of the existing house as a small roof pavilion.

Linking the new with the old, a ninety-foot-long undulating plaster wall both invites and denies communication between the public and private spaces. Set around the curve of the wall and the site, both the old and new wings focus on the dis-

tant views.

Spaces within the home are delineated through structural and sculptural elements—a studio is elevated on four posts which form the canopy chamber for a bed below, and a telescoping cone of bonderized steel forms a fireplace that functions as an eddy within the spatial flow.

The materials reinforce the variety of forms. A gridded rectilinear studio perched highest on the site is covered in cedar plywood with redwood battens. The master bedroom has curved walls and a skewed, vaulted roof, all clad with bonderized

sheet-metal panels. Service areas are finished in metal-troweled plaster. Tongue and groove wooden siding on the street facade recalls the existing lapped siding of house and fence.

Entry is signified by a small pool-shaped garden—a gesture of welcome in the arid Los Angeles climate. A tilting steel-and-glass canopy shades the street terrace and the visitor. The entry also serves as the center of movement throughout the site—a place from which one can proceed to the garden or the house, to a formal or informal order, to a public or private domain.

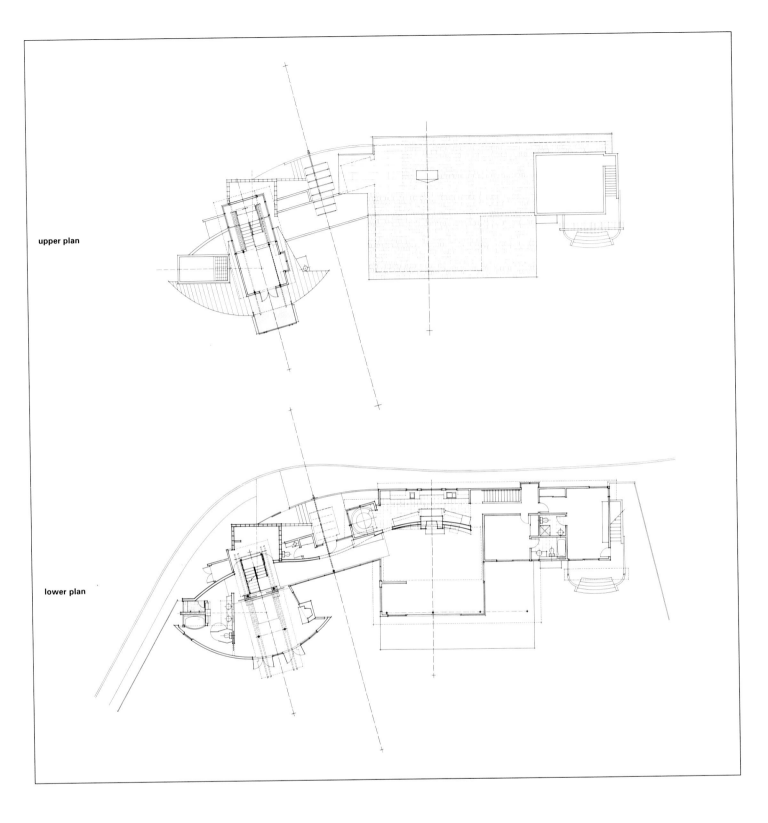

upper plan

lower plan

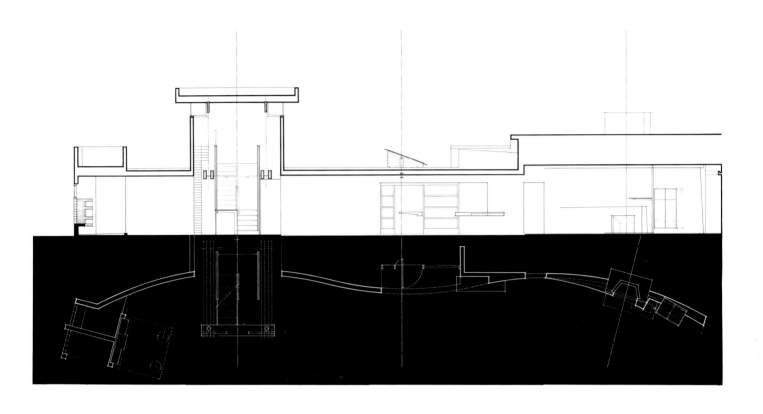

above: curvilinear wall,
section, plan
right: site plan

speedway cafe |

Venice, California   1991

Designed on a shoestring budget, the Speedway Cafe recently opened off the boardwalk in Venice. Essentially a small coffee house, the project represents our first venture into restaurant design and into a "roadside" architecture of signage and seduction.

If a dominant typology exists in Los Angeles architecture, the restaurant is a strong contender. Direct and unpretentious, the Speedway Cafe does not follow the pattern of "fashion statements" cre-

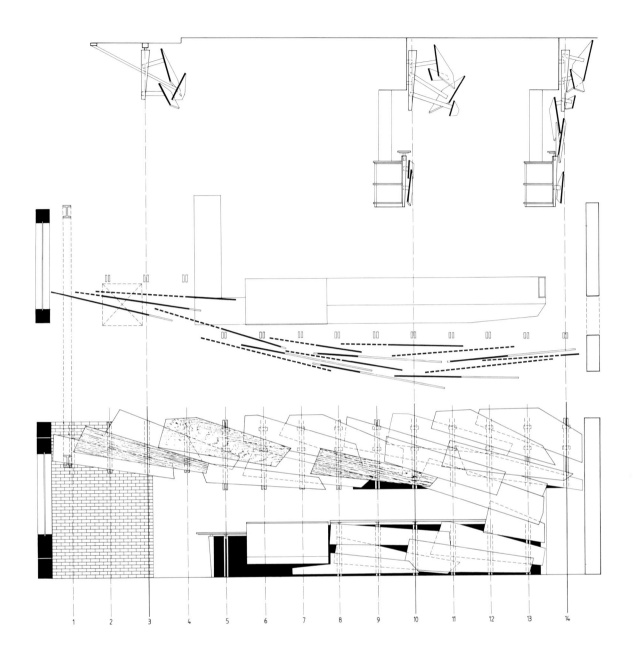

ated recently for a number of cutting-edge, west-side eateries. Creating another "new world order" for a high-end restaurant seemed ludicrous in light of the project's requirements.

This is not to say that the Speedway Cafe is understated in its approach. Large, rust-red billboard letters above a field of mustard yellow announce the nature of the establishment. Two huge square windows clad in galvanized metal wreak havoc with the scale of the street facade. Sited along the new Windward Avenue corridor in Venice, the cafe eventually may encounter a number of competitors

and thus a primary concern of the owner was distinctive visibility.

The vibrancy of the cafe's exterior hues contrasts with the tonal and material modulation of the interior. Once inside, a complex weave of cantilevered birchwood panels creates a series of dynamic cross sections. Supporting these planes, a trusswork of tapered Douglas fir beams establishes the structural cadence of the space in tight three-foot intervals. The rich wood surfaces stand in contrast to the cafe's steel bar and the kitchen's stainless-steel machinery. A strategy of contrast

also dictated the use of shiny white tiles in the kitchen to play against the flat finish of the concrete-slab floor.

Aside from the occasional grand gesture, the design focused on a clarity of detail and a rigorous attention to the operational needs of the client. Although the layout maximizes the seating within the existing structure, we left enough clearance above and at the bar to insure one never feels cramped within the space.

above: baffling studies

tisch-av<u>net</u>

Culver City, California 1991

Completed in the spring of 1991, Tisch-Avnet is among the latest and most refined of our office interiors. Just a stone's throw away from MGM, these offices for a team of producers were installed in an existing four-story structure.

A steel-and-glass canopy extends to the exterior from the three-story lobby, creating a new entrance for the building. While filling the lobby, the canopy extends from the ground level up into the producer's office level and the associate's level

above it. Set at an angle that follows the line of movement from the street into the main level of the building, the axis is terminated vertically by an oculus that aligns with a tunnel leading to a three-story conference room. The oculus also fills the third-floor reception space with natural light.

The reception area is defined and contained by a sloping curved wall made of troweled and colored stucco. This wall forms the backdrop to the reception area and is interrupted by the tunnel leading to the conference room. This room is hooded by a pair of sixteen-foot-high truncated walls sus-

pended from a wood-and-steel structure. Constructed of sandblasted Plexiglass, the walls absorb the natural light from the ceiling skylight and the artificial light from fluorescent fixtures located behind them.

We customized the executive offices for each of the three producers. Colors, materials, and furnishings were fashioned according to each producer's particular tastes, creating a varied set of spaces and designs.

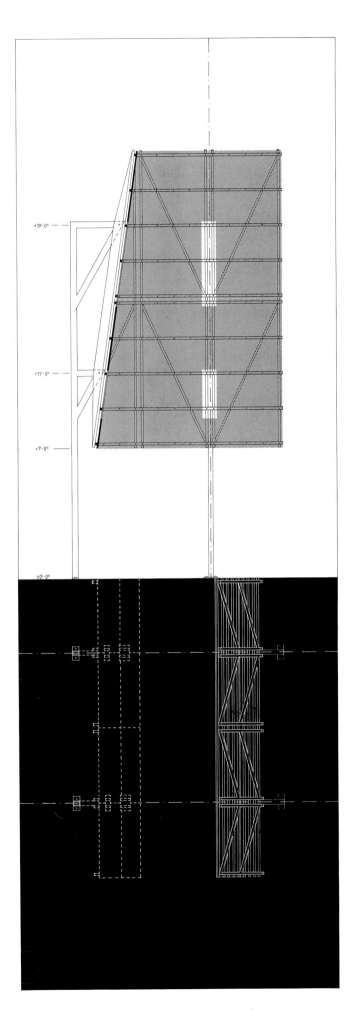

detail, conference canopy

    **plaster colors**

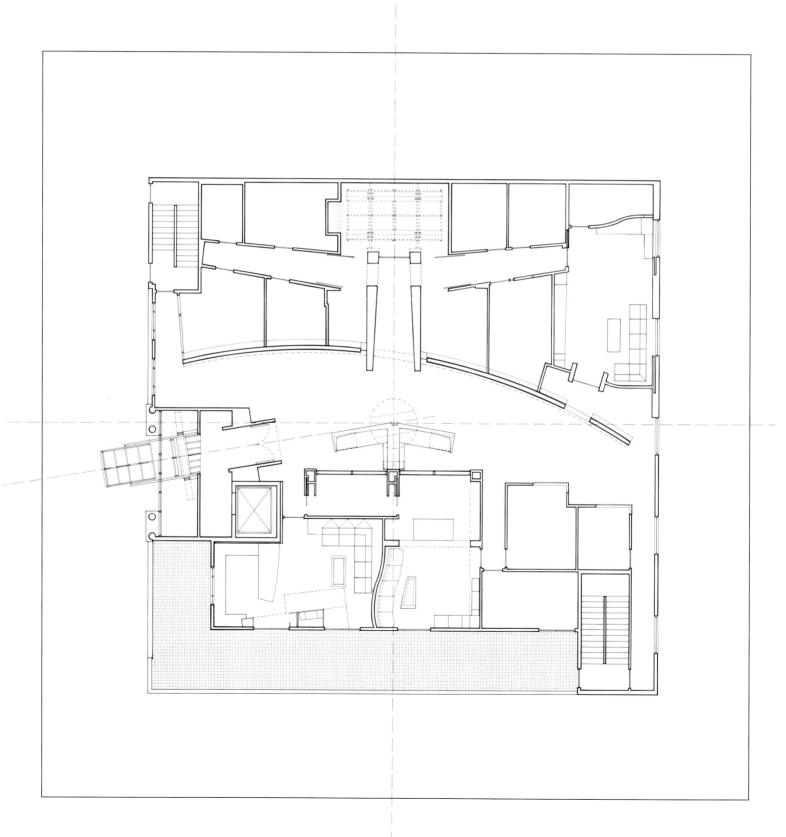

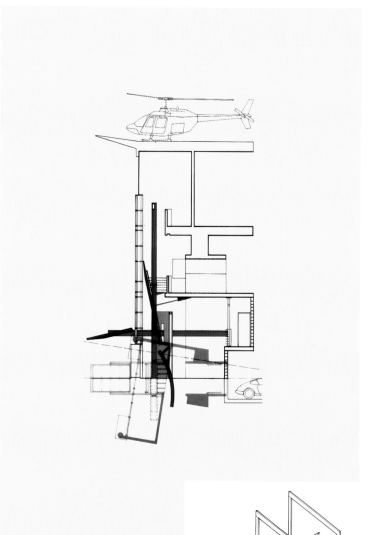

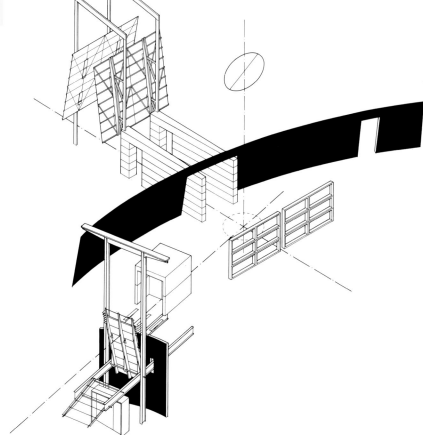

top: entrance section
lower right: sequential isometric

divine design pavilion |

Santa Monica, California   1991

The Divine Design Pavilion was built for a design show held at the Santa Monica Airport. Rising up in the middle of a vacated airplane hangar, the pavilion became the centerpiece of the show.

A sculptural piece as much as an architectural intervention, the pavilion required little in the way of program. Divine Design needed a place to show and sell their clothing, so we created a dense perimeter of fir framing with regular bays suitable for either hanging or shelving their products. Once this shell was erected, a yellow service island was inserted as an anchor for all the commercial functions of the pavilion.

The abstract form of the pavilion plays on a number of precedents, resembling at once an inverted ark and the ubiquitous Gehry fish installations. The more immediate models, however, were in the hull-shaped forms of the Propaganda, Raznick, and Kaplan projects.

The pavilion departs from each of these sources in a number of critical respects. The structural system has been left exposed and clearly refers more to the the structure of wooden boat hulls than to the standardized construction methods of Gehry's fish installations. Carefully ordered and finished, the fir armature can stand alone as an environmental sculpture.

Just as important are the sandblasted fiberglass sheets that "scale" the pavilion—one side rising up from the floor plane as the other descends—and convolute a uniform reading of the whole. The translucent sheathing also throws any nautical metaphors into question, evoking images of flight rather than mere flotation.

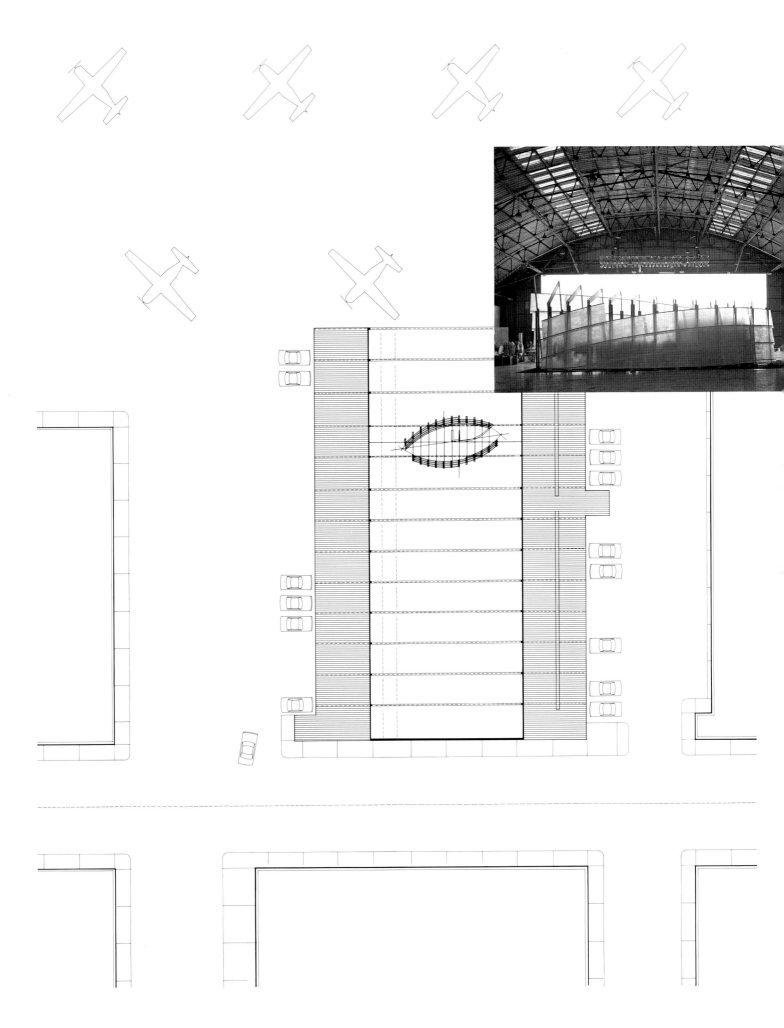

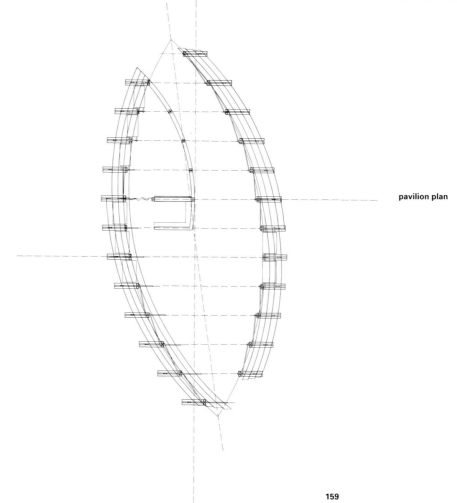

pavilion plan

limelight productions |

Los Angeles, California   1991

The Limelight Productions project involved the re-modeling of a large double-bay warehouse space in Hollywood. As in the Propaganda Films project, the space was encapsulated by series of bow-string trusses arrayed along two matched bays. A compact site and limited budget set many of the parameters for this commission.

Much of the design focused on the careful articulation of an entrance sequence beginning outside the building's western wall and continuing through the entire length of the interior. Playing on the Corbusian precedent at the Villa Stein, a canti-levered *brise-soleil*—now torqued and expanding out in forced perspective—signifies the entrance to the offices. Once inside, a canted wall trans-forms into a long low canopy that defines the re-ception area, while a backlit shield totem of translu-cent fiberglass concludes the east end of the axis. To moderate the lighting of this corridor, we em-ployed a freestanding baffling wall to fragment the rays from skylights above.

Following the established pattern of the truss-work above, we lined the perimeter of the space with individual offices that surround a "pool" of assistants' stations. Broadly reinterpreting Frank Lloyd Wright's model work spaces in the Larkin Building and the Johnson Wax Headquarters, these composite desk arrangements become al-most sculptural elements symbolizing a new ad-ministrative network for the company.

Conference rooms and public spaces were con-centrated near the entrance so that the visitor would perceive a complex far larger than it actually is. The grandeur of the long entrance arcade, com-

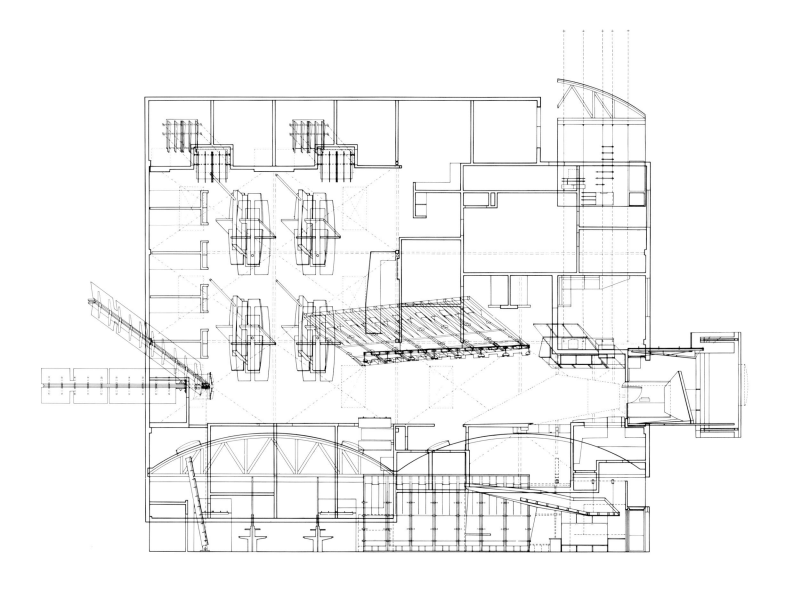

above: plan, section, axonometric
below: longitudinal section

facing page:
top left: lightwall section, elevation plan
far right: entrance plan and axonometric

bined with the exploded scale of the assistants' stations, appear to anticipate a large multimedia empire, when in fact Limelight is scaled within the tight confines of reason.

A consistent logic was applied to materials, details, and color scheme. Birch plywood was used in all cabinetry. The edges of the laminated materials were exposed or stacked to celebrate their materiality. Aluminium elements—fasteners, joints, wall bases, hardware, and sheeting— were introduced as structural supports and serve as the only embellishments of an otherwise utilitarian office interior.

Glass and fiberglass provide a light-transforming counterbalance to the otherwise opaque composition.

Material and color selection proved more positively influential than we had first expected. As one moves through the completed space, the tactile collages of brick, wood, aluminium, glass, and fiberglass reinforce one another powerfully, as does the range of matte yellow, blue, bright white, brick-red, and natural wood-grain colors.

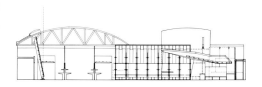

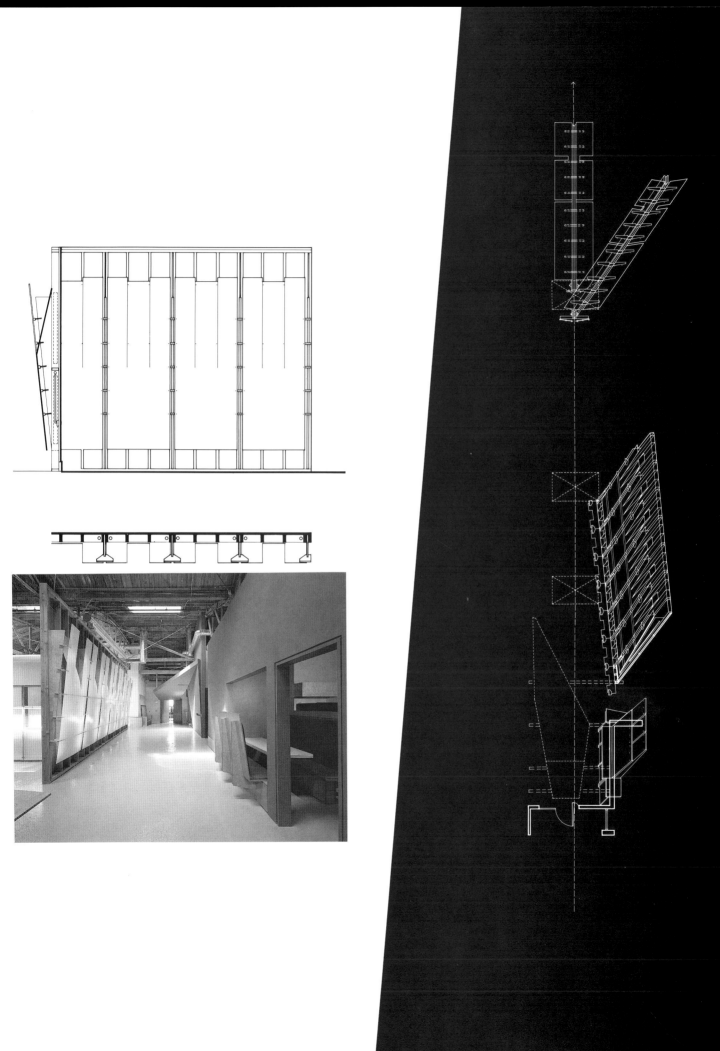

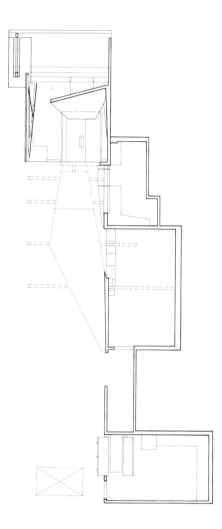

entrance sequence: sectional elevation and plan

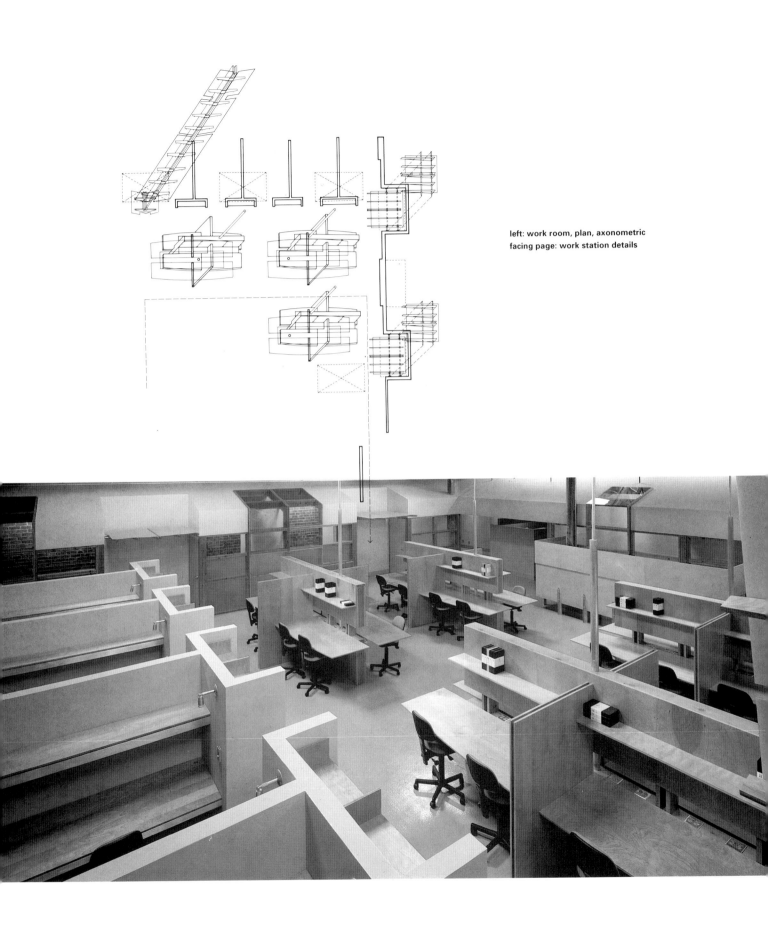

left: work room, plan, axonometric
facing page: work station details

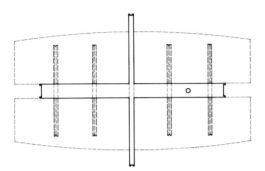

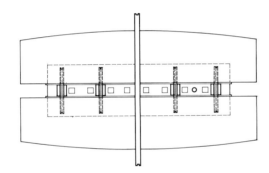

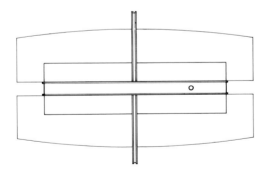

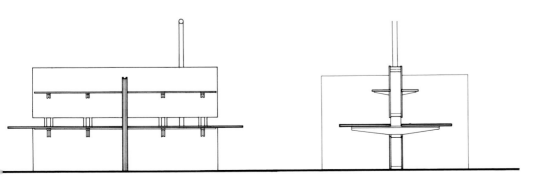

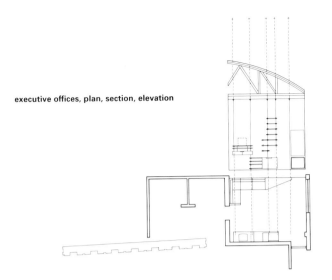

executive offices, plan, section, elevation

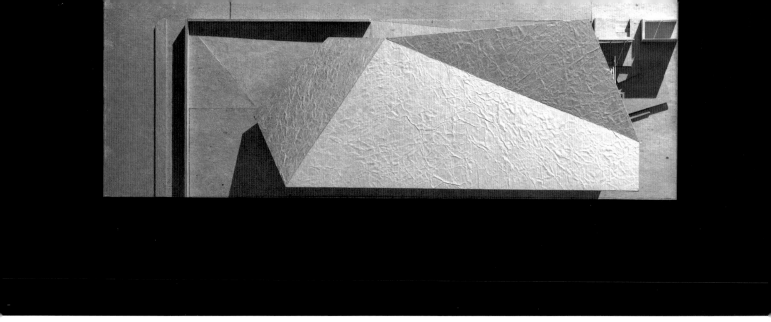

facing page: cross and longitudinal sections

sydney and susan baldwin house

Venice, California 1992

This beach house in Venice actually consists of two houses that abut a small street and an alleyway a few blocks from the ocean. Designed for a photographer and his family, the Baldwin House also includes a two-bedroom rental unit. Electric Avenue, the original cable car access to Venice by the Sea, still cuts a wide swath through the area, fifty feet to the east of the Baldwin site. As at Bright and Associates, the Baldwin acknowledges the larger urban condition: the entrance is cut away at a 40-degree angle parallel to that of Electric Avenue.

The two-story studio space sits across the street from Bright and Associates, and pays homage to that project by using many of the same materials. The rental unit is accessed from a private garden in the rear of the site, and the entire complex is unified by a large, sweeping sheet-metal roof. The metal panels will be made of anodized titanium to achieve the iridescence akin to the skin of a reptile or fish. This gesture acknowledges the home's proximity to the sea and imbues it with a sense of grandeur appropriate to the site.

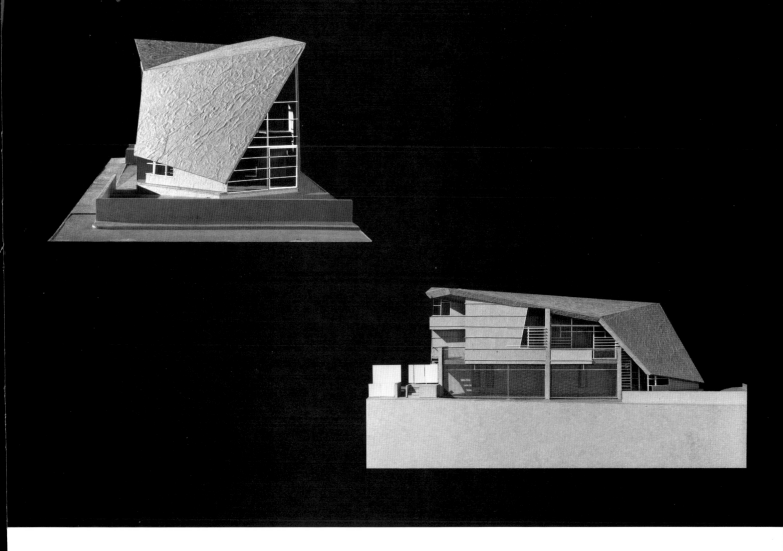

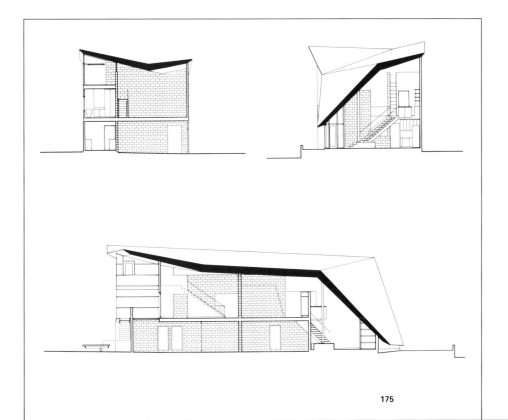

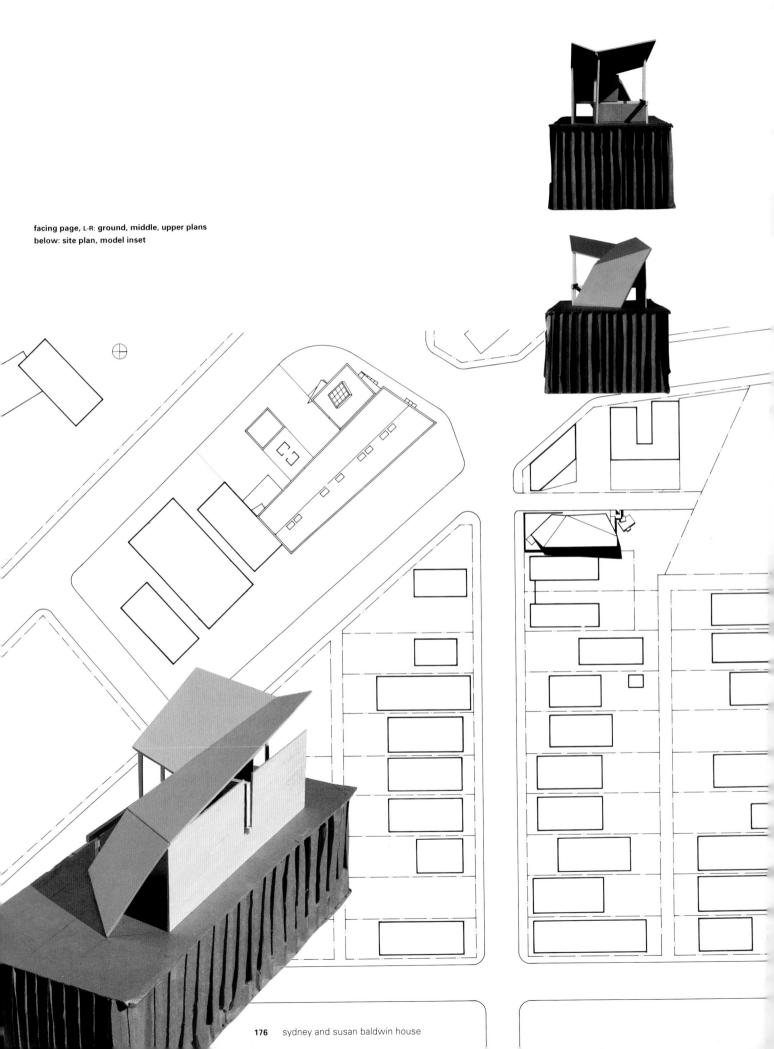

facing page, L-R: **ground, middle, upper plans**
below: **site plan, model inset**

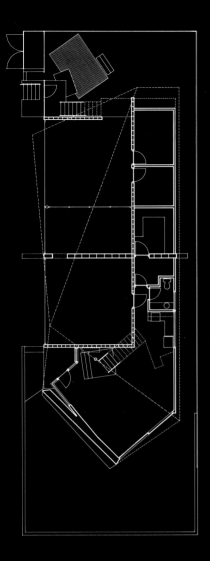

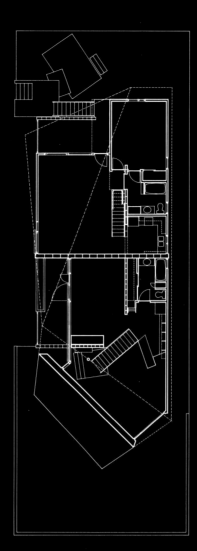

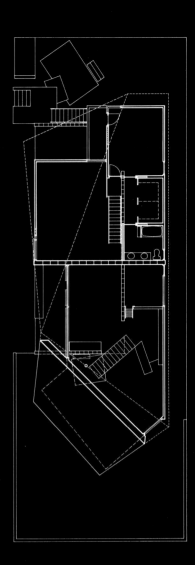

To support the vast roof, two major masonry walls cut through the plan, dividing the interior into two units, and into service and served spaces with each. The down-turning sweep of the roof shelters the largest of the interior spaces from the south light to provide a studio for the photographer. The cruciform structure of the two primary walls is sculpted away in places to modulate movement and light, and the ground slab is gently terraced up from the voided entrance. Darkroom, baths, and storage are stacked along the north side up to three levels and enclosed by a light skin of wood and metal paneling. Glass infill windows close the reveals between roofing and paneling systems, insuring that each reads independent of the other.

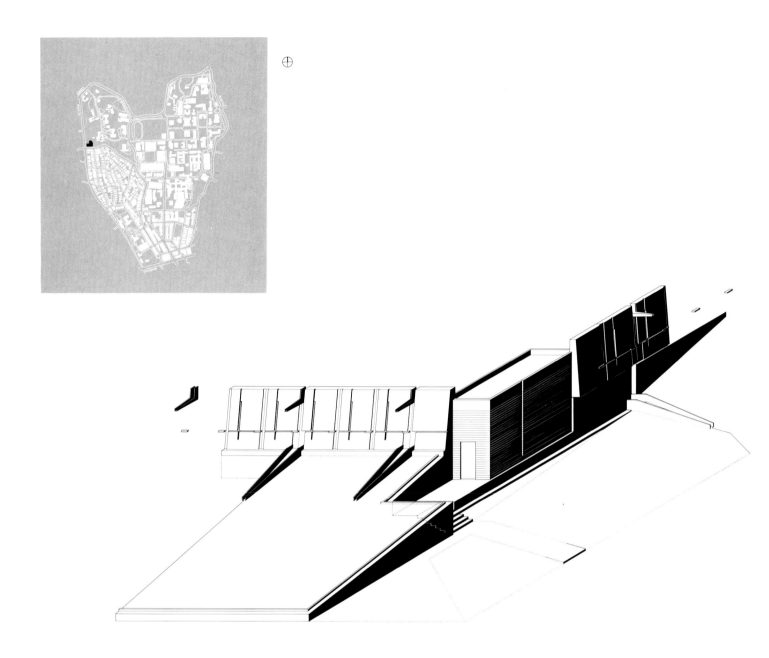

ucla southern regional library

Westwood, California   1991

The Southern Regional Library Project at UCLA is situated on the western edge of the UCLA campus, adjacent to the residential community of Veteran and Gayley Avenues.

Sunk into the earth, our addition forms a base block to the original structure. The building volume is further concealed by an earth berm sloping up from Veteran Avenue. Together, the berm and the building create a terrace on which the original library is positioned. Brick, concrete and metal are fashioned together to create a building which blends into the landscape.

Brick is the material of linkage. It complements the more formal buildings of center campus, articulates the joints between the original library and our addition, and outlines the edges of the site. The building mass reveals itself as a one-story plinth clad in precast concrete panels. Designed as a series of vertical subdivisions, these panels contrast with the horizontality of the original structure.

Steel scuppers are scribed into the vertical walls of the terrace and are echoed by concrete channels which cut into the earth berm below. A steel trellis covered with foliage softly veils the Gayley Avenue elevation, breaking down the mass of the addition's southern edge and providing it with pedestrian scale.

This project is a building as landscape. Time is an important factor. As the foliage increases and covers the addition, the delineation of one element from the other will be emphasized. Also, a sense of the base block as a buffer for the western edge of the campus will be augmented.

facing page:
top left: UCLA campus site plan
center: partial isometric

top: side elevation
center: site section
bottom: *details*, concrete panel

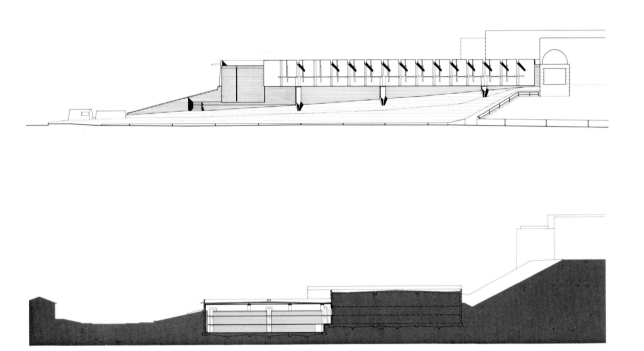

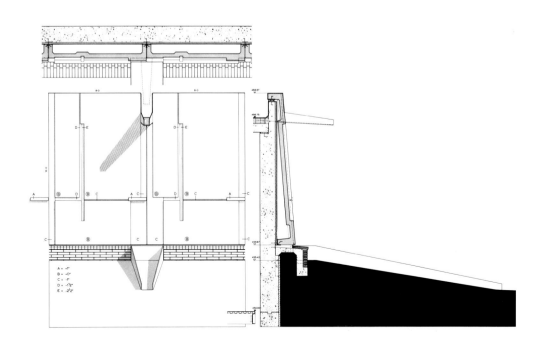

model, **rear view**

john tesh house

Mar Vista, California   1991

A small home high in the bluffs of Mar Vista, the John Tesh House frames a series of panoramic views of the Pacific Ocean. The home's winged design followed, in part, from the relatively large fitness, studio, and study facilities requested by the client. Zoning ordinances, on the other hand, compelled us to keep the design oriented around the home's lap pool and rear court.

In order to maximize the incredible site, we sought to control the perspective and points-of-view as much as possible, re-presenting nature in views ranging from the panoramic to the periscopic. To this end, the house employs an L-shape with a three-story entry tower, thus extending as far as possible along the x, y, and z coordinates of an imagined Cartesian grid.

A public zone contains an auto court, garage, sound studio, study, and living and dining areas. A private arm contains the master bedroom suite, fitness facilities, and a solarium. While one could interpret the structure as a series of light boxes or *camerae obscurae,* the house is more fully articu-lated in architectural terms. The rooms run a complex architectural gamut from open and light, almost Miesian spaces, to closed, cool masonry enclosures. The vertical extension over the entrance alludes to the tradition of bell towers in Spanish architecture, encasing a delicate spiral stairway that leads up to the most dramatic view. At the same time, the tower expands and opens into an almost facial configuration. Taken as a whole, the anthropomorphic composition of the house begins to suggest a seated, meditating figure looking sedately out over the ocean.

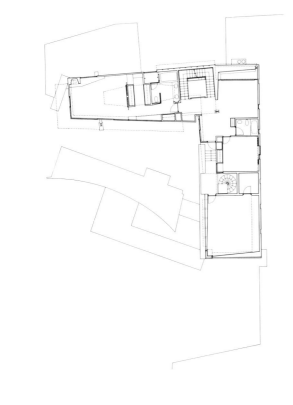

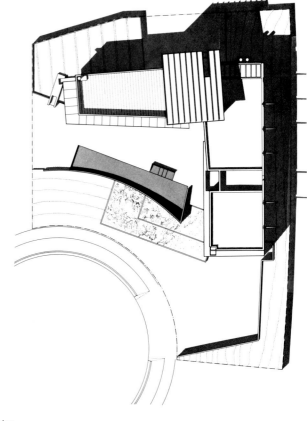

second floor roof plan

first floor | third floor

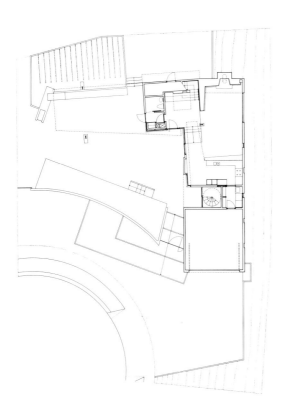

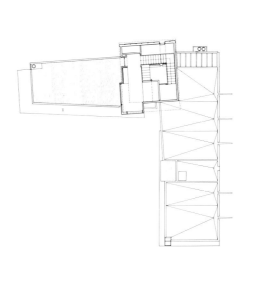

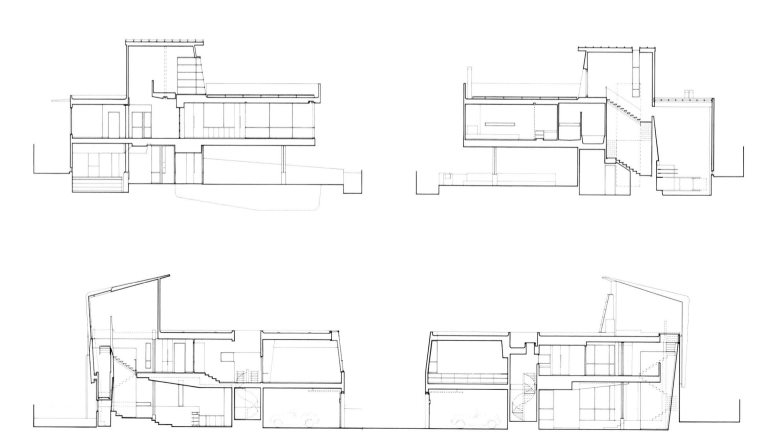

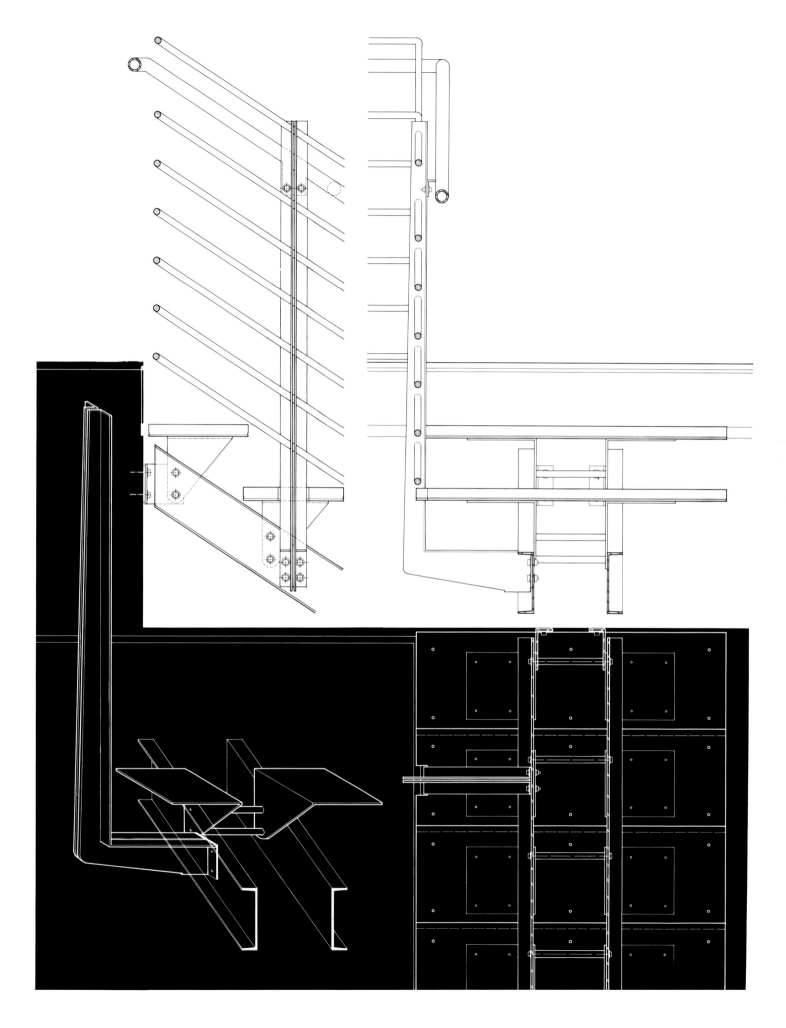

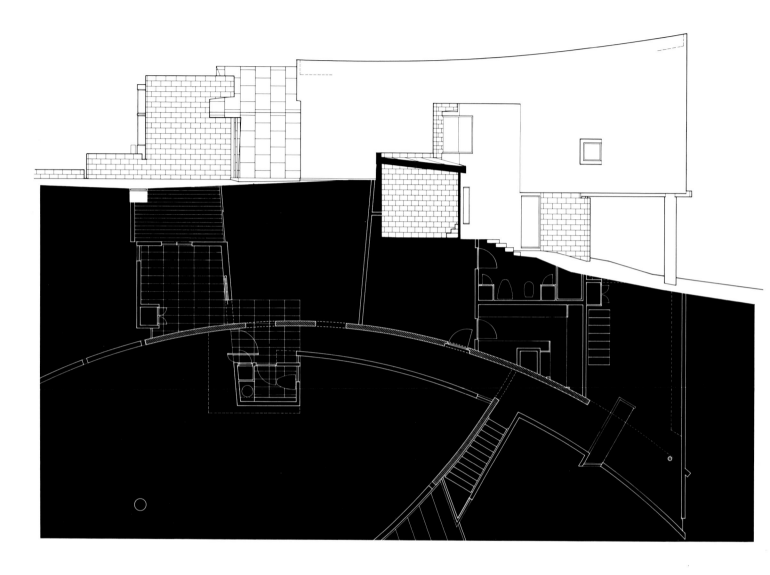

kaplan house

Malibu, California 1991

The Kaplan House serves not one but two families. Situated in the rolling hills of Malibu, among native chaparral and wild grasses, the home is oriented toward the mountains and the sea. It consists of two related wings: one for a writer, his two young sons, and professional wife; and another for his mother, a painter. Together the two homes enclose an elliptical courtyard, sited along an axis binding the mountains to the sea. The northern terminus of the axis is Point Dume, which also forms

the northern tip of Santa Monica Bay. There is a 180° view of the ocean from the site.

The upper floor of the large house contains the living room and master bedroom. It is elevated above the ground for views over the small house. The children's bedrooms are on the courtyard level and are accessible to the play area, which includes a croquet court. The lowest level contains guest bedrooms and a passage to the mother's house. The small house is a self-contained bungalow of one level, with a curved gallery for displaying art that terminates in a lofty studio lit by

clerestory windows. A terrace overlooking Point Dume was added so the artist can work indoors or out. Two curving walls of concrete block shape the inner court and form the principal structure of both houses. These walls also define the structural and sculptural elements that form the home's living spaces.

The houses were designed to be relatively inexpensive, both in construction and maintenance. Their spaces are straightforward, even informal, as are the materials: rough-sawn plywood panels; asphalt roofing; exposed, sandblasted concrete

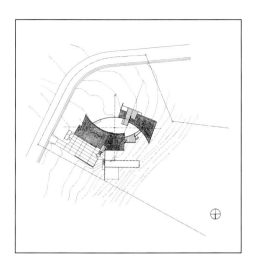

above: site plan
right, bottom to top:
lower, ground, and upper plans

facing page:
mother's house, section,
elevation, plan

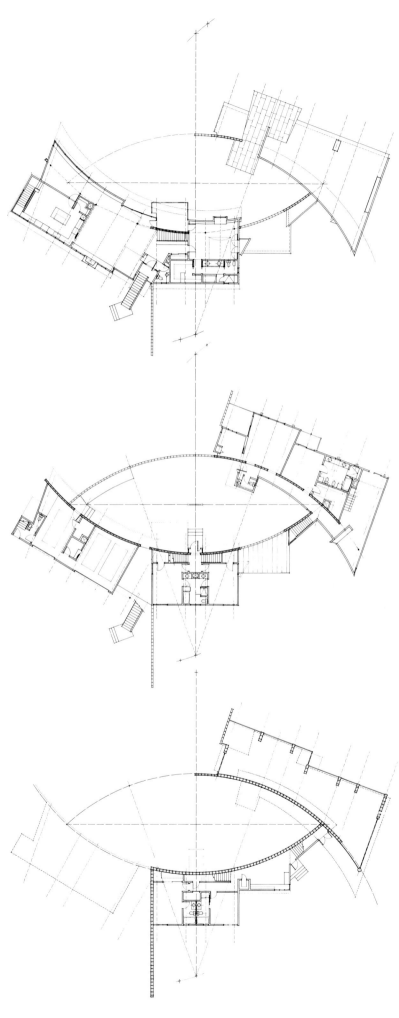

block; bonderized sheet metal; and stucco. Decks
are redwood with steel and cable railings.

To preserve the spirit of the site and its sense
of isolation, as well as to provide protection from
the prevailing winds, the two homes are nestled
into the slopes, and are terraced with the site up to
the north. As much of the site as possible is left untouched.

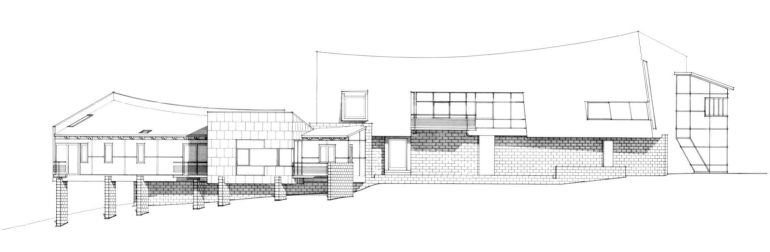

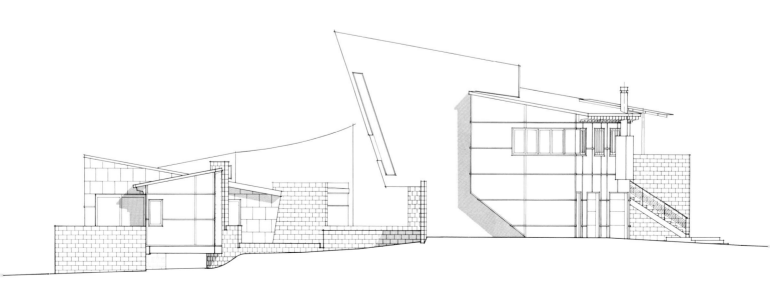

facing page:
model and elevations

below: main house, cross sections
and ground plan

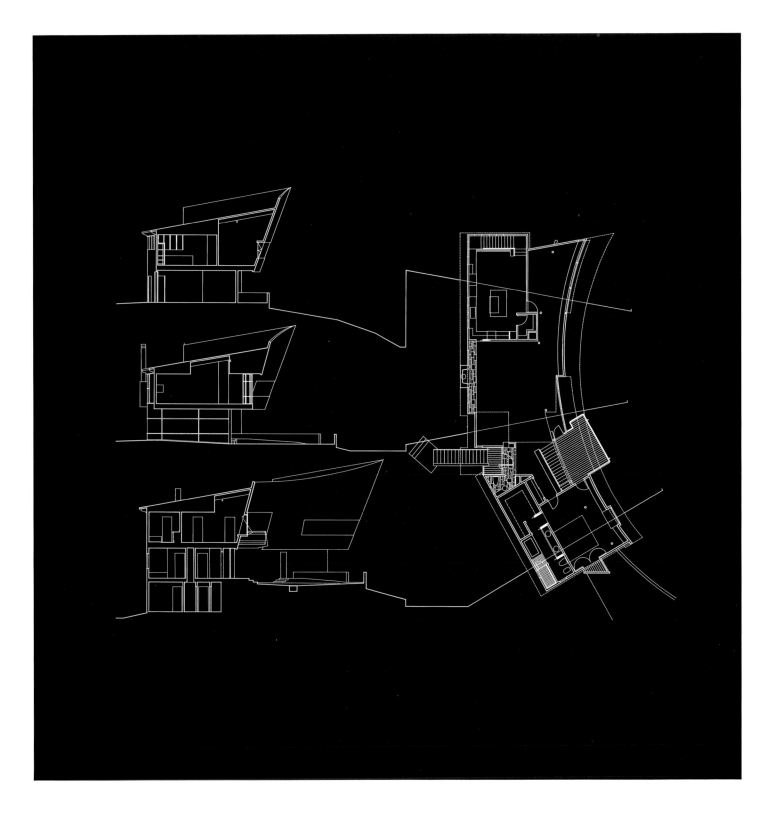

hague house |

The Hague, The Netherlands 1992

This small 1,800-square-foot house is one of eight detached garden houses to be built in a suburban area of The Hague. Organized on five separate levels, the house opens up at the ground level to a split-level garden. From here the building winds around from the entry to the rear facade with a stepped terrace connecting the various bedroom levels. Upon entering, a small vestibule is provided to shed one's boots; the entry path then leads along a walkway to the kitchen and dining area. Be-

low, the living room opens out onto the garden through large picture windows. The studio above is a suspended platform which looks down upon the living area. Two levels of bedrooms occupy the upper portion of the building.

Built of brick, steel, and wood, the house pays homage to the early-twentieth-century garden cottages at Park Neerwijk. These somewhat idiosyncratic buildings combine a wide assortment of materials into a set of garden pavilions that resemble a set of chess pieces on a contoured board.

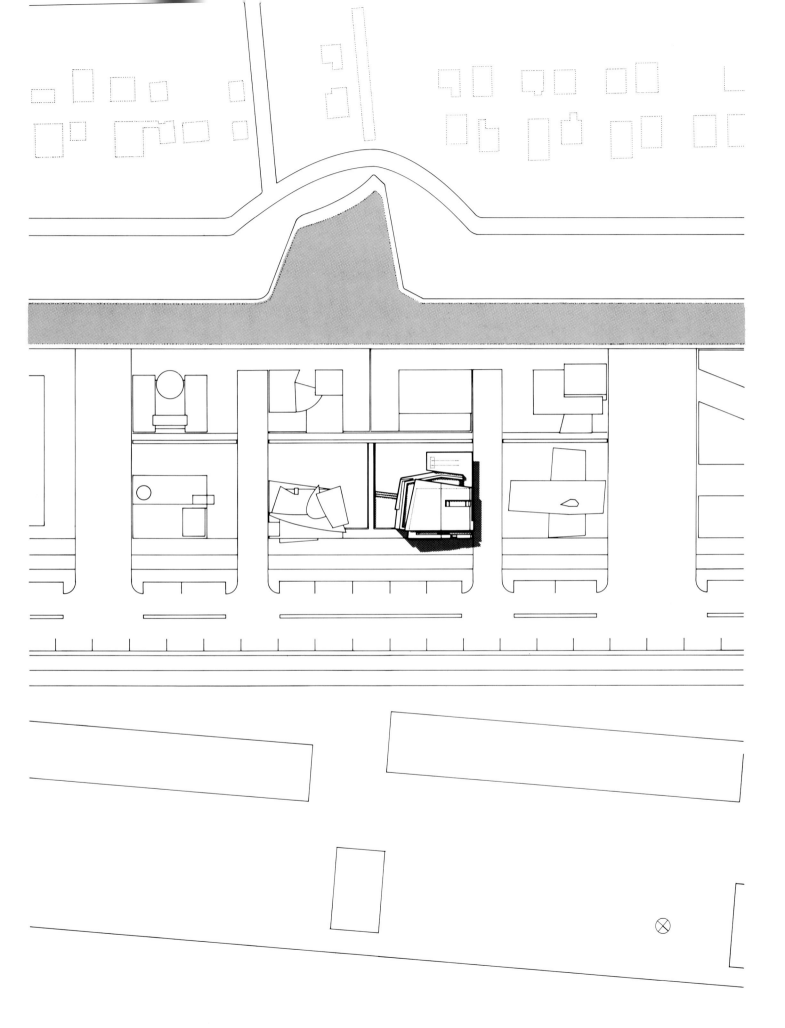

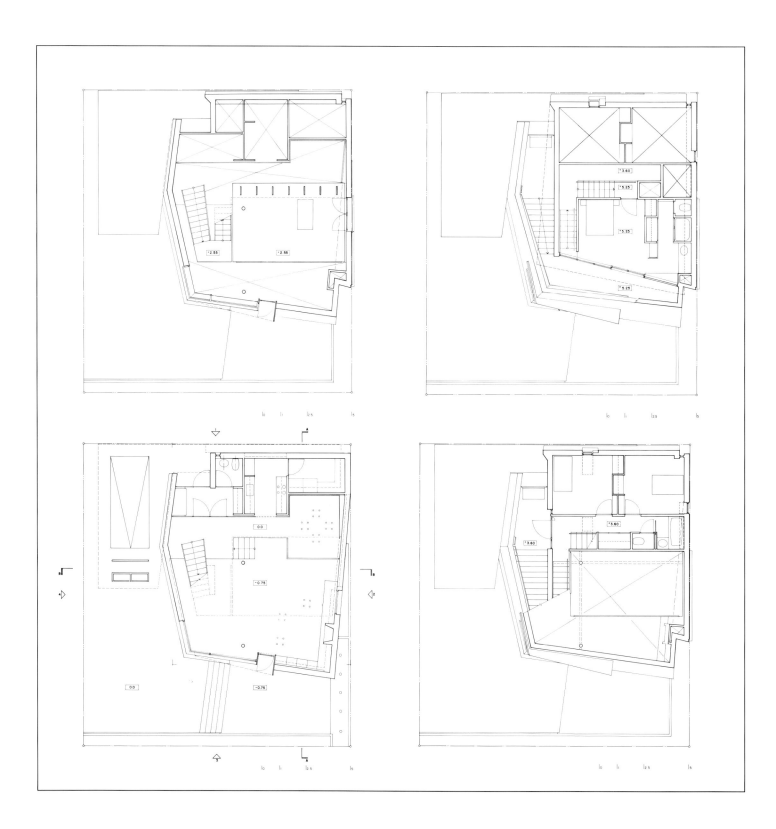

facing page:
top L-R: **second and fourth floor plans**
bottom L-R: **first and third floor plans**
below: *models*

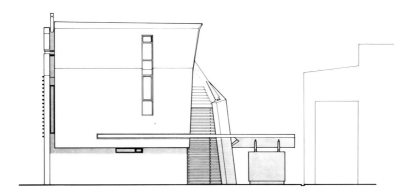

elevations

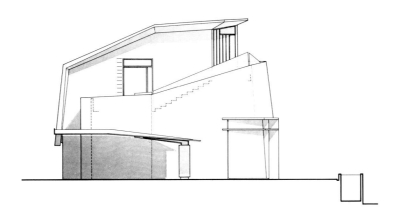

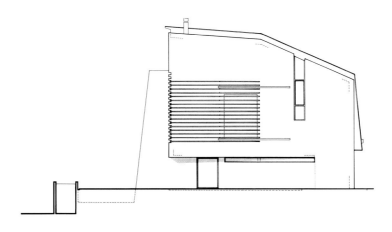

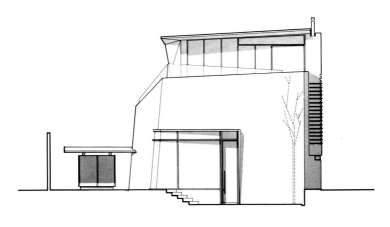

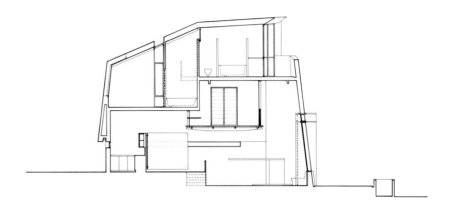

model, side view and sections

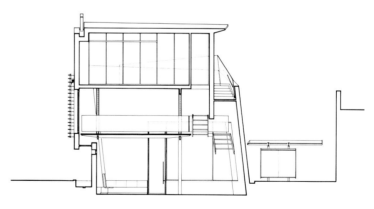

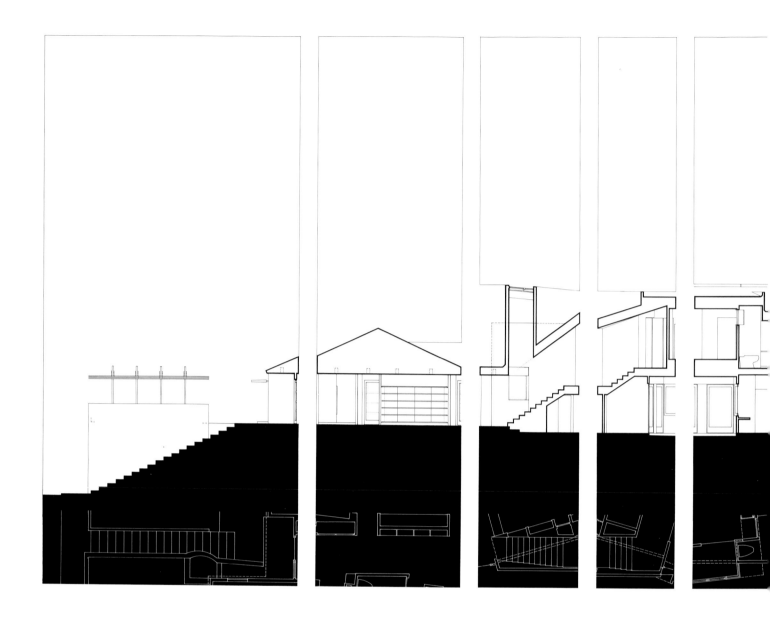

woo pavilion

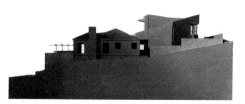

Silverlake, California   1992

A 1,400-foot addition to a bungalow on the north side of Silverlake, the Woo Pavilion adds a few new dimensions to the notion of a "Pavilion in a Garden." As in the Lamy-Newton project, the addition is to be shielded from the street and at a dramatic conceptual remove from the original home.

The clients needed to expand the original home in a number of ways, principally to contain their ever-expanding collection of books and to provide an "original" environment for them. This intriguing combination of concerns gave rise to our scheme, in which hundreds of feet of bookshelves are integrated into a dramatic passageway, creating a new kind of generative space for the Woos. This "literary" passageway offers the family ready access to human experience of the past and present.

One reaches the addition through a new axis cut through the original house. The axis runs at a slightly oblique angle from the front door to the new structure in the rear. In addition to the axis, a patio and pergola in front of the home and a few slight modifications to the existing streetside

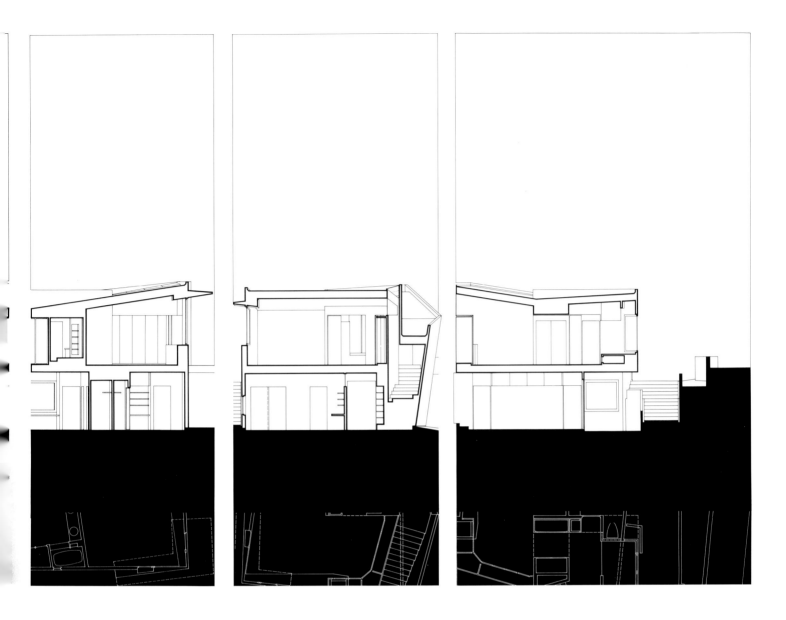

garage were the only changes in the existing structure. The addition creates three new bedrooms, two on the first floor and a new master bedroom on the second. Bath and storage spaces were added on both levels as well.

The library-hallway runs along one edge of the two lower rooms and then up a curving stairway—modeled after a nautilus shell—to the master suite. A glowing lightwell over the staircase draws one up to the second-floor spaces and sheds light on the stairway and bookshelves (without damaging the volumes).

The upper level of the addition was conceived as a total retreat for the Woos, with a beautiful view of Lake Silverlake and an abundance of natural light. The major space, the largest in the house, is a master bedroom and studio with a large corner window. In addition to a private balcony, moveable storage walls were introduced to provide greater flexibility to the space.

We tried to reflect the gentle and enlightened philosophy of the clients in the exterior disposition of the pavilion and in its placement on the site. The pavilion was pulled to one side of the property, im-

proving its view of Silverlake and allowing an open, outdoor "room" on the other side. Clad in stone-dashed stucco, the walls of the addition appear to buckle and pull away in places, revealing—and illuminating—an interior world.

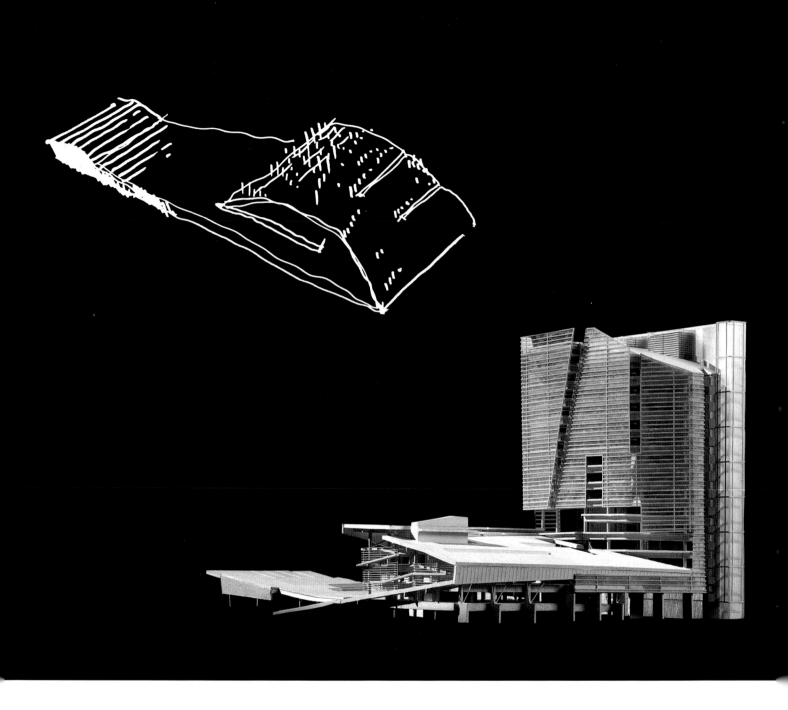

bunka shutter and the new industrial city

Tokyo, Japan 1992

A city within, and on the edge, this commission is divided into two phases. A "New Industrial City" is proposed, comprising offices, laboratories, and studios for architects and graphic and industrial designers, sited along the northern perimeter of Tokyo.

Central to this plan is the Metro Station, from which visitors descend into a series of public spaces enclosed and defined by galleries, shops, restaurants, and cafes. Less formal than other urban projects in Tokyo, the New Industrial City borrows the open-air logic of the original Cité Industrielle of Tony Garnier, taking advantage of its proximity to a landscaped hillside park and a planted river basin of the Tokyo River. The design extends these landscape features into the plan as a series of terraced platforms which in turn become the base for a series of office blocks along the main vehicular corridor of the site.

The headquarters for Bunka Shutter, a prominent Japanese building products company, crown the design. This semi-transparent tower sits on a garden platform that includes studios, laboratories, and other facilities integral to the operations of the company. Actual products of the company are utilized in facade and in plan to transform the tower into a catalogued "billboard" for Bunka Shutter. These components, such as window shutters and overhead doors, highlight the design and affirm the graceful precision of the company and its products. They create a kinetic building which changes according to the location of the sun at different times of the day and the year.

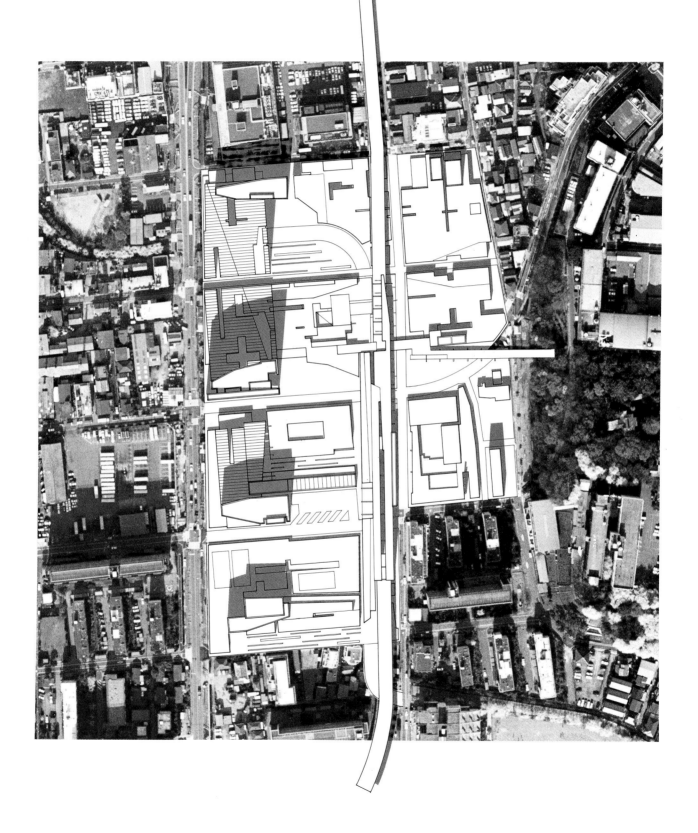

facing page:
top left: concept sketch
bottom right: *model,*
Bunka office building

below:
urban design site plan

ucla installation II

Westwood, California   1991

In the fall of 1991, this was our second installation at the UCLA School of Architecture. It represents an "Architect's Room," and counters our earlier exhibits at UCLA and the Walker Art Center. These earlier pieces acted as didactic expositions of what architecture might become. The viewer was led through spaces that "taught" a future for architecture. The installations assumed an architectonic stature, so that while viewing the exhibits one inhabited spaces as determinant as those represent-

ed in the images and models on display.

The second UCLA installation, however, tries to capture the process of creating and making. Neither a futuristic vision of work to come nor a realistic portrayal of architectural practice (i.e., office production), this exhibit seeks to freeze a moment of genesis, while propounding the paradox that no such moment can be captured and contained.

In the "Architect's Room" the instruments and accoutrements of making are hopelessly intermingled with that which is made. A drafting table, strewn with drawing equipment and stacked high

with models in various states of disrepair, stands amidst loose drawings and sketches pinned-up erratically or fallen to the floor.

As in the work of Ed Kienholz, our installation poses an alternative "reality" in which the standard hierarchy of the senses does not apply. This approximates the irreality of creative development in which much of the perceivable world simply falls away. The "Architect's Room" searches for the lost retreat of the architect, as a Kienholz image might capture the exact aroma of a prostitute's Las Vegas hotel room.

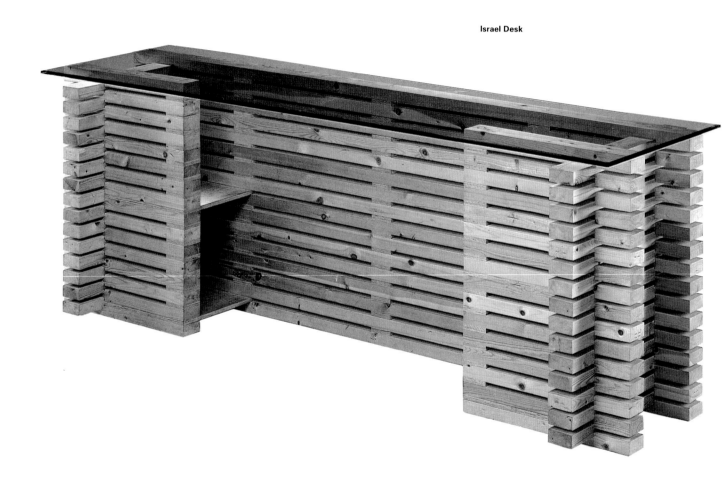

Israel Desk

furniture and furnishings

Floor and Table Lamps, 1981
Floating Tables, 1986
Salt and Pepper Shakers and
Stainless Candlesticks, 1988
*Israel Desk and T.V. Cabinet,*1988
Tisch Coffee Table, 1991
Limelight Conference Table, 1991
Limelight Executive Desk, 1991

The Israel Desk and TV Cabinets were designed using the two-by-four stacking technique first explored in the Walker Art Center exhibit installation. As we experimented with different "weaves" to form the wall units in the Walker show, I realized that the same patterns of joinery could be applied to furniture designs. Here, the wood members are quarter-lapped for strength with interstitial spaces left for cantilevered plywood shelving.

The Tisch Coffee Table and the tables for Limelight Productions were designed to complement their particular interiors.

The lamps are referenced to an earlier Zen philosophy of design, hence the rock.

The Floating Tables were designed for the Altman House in Malibu. Both tables were fabricated in steel, one with a wooden box infill frame, the other with a copper-plated steel box. The top of both tables is plate glass over iridescent glass, which matches the pivoting transom in the home's skylight stairtower.

Limelight executive desk

Limelight conference table

top left: shelf and curtains by David James

Floating Tables

Floor and Table Lamps

below: stainless steel salt
and pepper shakers, plans, elevations
facing page:
stainless steel candlesticks, plans, elevations

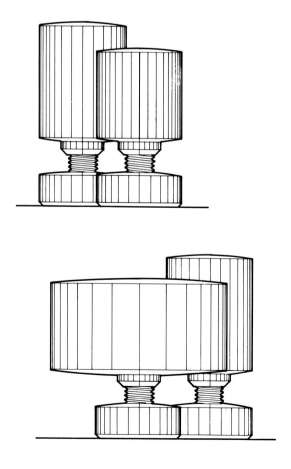

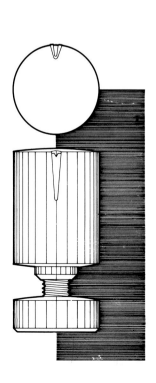

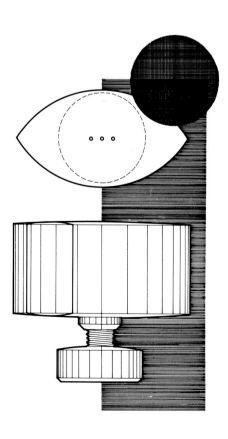

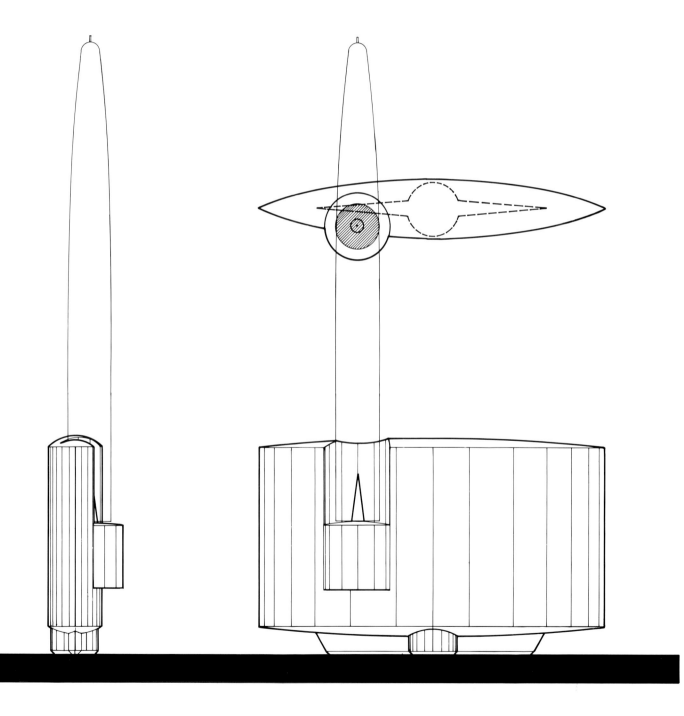

takeoff: the journey of frank israel

Thomas S. Hines

In his classic essay, "The Stages of Economic Growth," written in 1964, economist Walt Whitman Rostow posited a cyclical explanation of economic development that has subsequently been applied to many other phenomena. Rostow's five stages include: first, "the traditional society"; second, "the pre-conditions for takeoff"; third, "the takeoff"; fourth, "the drive to maturity"; and fifth, "the age of high mass consumption." This now-familiar paradigm is also applicable to individual experiences of life and work as in, for example, the progression of Frank Israel.[1]

By the late 1980s and early 1990s, a period rich with significant commissions—from the Lamy-Newton, Arango-Berry, Goldberg-Bean, and Robert Altman residences to the studios for Bright and Associates, Propaganda Films, Virgin Records, and Limelight Films—Frank Israel has obviously been on a roll. Following the traditional nurturing of childhood and of "pre-takeoff," when he pondered and learned from the examples of others, he is now, in his early "takeoff," beginning to find his voice. His "drive to maturity" will follow this phase and will deepen and clarify an increasingly influential *oeuvre.*

In the mid-twentieth century, an earlier generation of architectural historians, such as George Kubler of Yale, argued that the biographical component—the evaluation of the development of the individual artistic psyche—was not intrinsically important and was, in fact, a counterproductive smokescreen in the proper study of the history of art. In the late twentieth century, however, that claim seems so fatuous that it hardly needs refutation. One does not have to be an orthodox Freudian to believe in the primacy of early psychic development as a contributing factor in human creativity. Neither does one have to be a doctrinaire Marxist to believe in the necessity of a contextual analysis of art and aesthetic theory. Tracing the education of a developing architect, and the "influence" of heroes, mentors, and contemporary colleagues, can shed light not only on an individual's subsequent work but, conversely, on the period of history that the individual has traversed. Journeys taken by different people through the same times and places naturally show similarities and affinities. Yet, because of personal and professional contingencies, all lives and journeys are unique and constitute experiences unlike any other.

Franklin David Israel has inhabited several worlds since his birth on December 2, 1945, in Brooklyn, New York. As he approached his forty–sixth birthday in 1991, he was certain that three early environments were crucial in shaping his development. The first was his hometown of Elizabeth, New Jersey, to which his parents had moved when he was a year old. Irving Isadore and Zelda Carr Israel, second-generation Americans of Romanian and Russian ancestry, owned a children's clothing store where Frank and his sister, Roslyn, worked part-time as they were growing up. Frank's only positive memory of the experience was observing and then working with the window dresser. The Israels first lived in an apartment above the store until they moved to a quasi-colonial house in the Elizabeth suburbs. As they became more prosperous, they also became avid golfers and Frank remembers himself as a golf orphan. It all added up to suburban claustrophobia.

The first significant respite was the eccentric, progressive, sports-centered Camp Tohone in the Berkshires, catering to an upper–middle-class Jewish clientele and presided over by Peter, Sarah, and Engels Menaker, the latter named for Frederick Engels, a patron saint of the leftist-oriented family. In the McCarthyite 1950s, the Menakers paid periodic visits to their Russian homeland and brought back slides and stories for their campers at Tohone. At nearby Tanglewood, they also introduced their charges to music and to their friend Aaron Copland who conducted there. Enamored of Copland, Frank finagled a part-time job with the master, trekking to Tanglewood twice a week to work as the composer's flunky. He admired Copland because, from a Russian-Jewish background, he had somehow created the quintessential American music: "Rodeo," "Appalachian Spring," "A Lincoln Portrait," "Billy the Kid." At age fourteen, Frank loved all of these compositions and could whistle the entirety of Copland's Third Symphony.

Tohone also stimulated Frank's environmental awareness and prompted the design of his first built structure, a log cabin, a primitive hut to house the camp newspaper, which he edited. In addition to the Menakers, Israel recalled, the place was full of bright, unconventional people, from fellow campers to staff counselors, who left a lasting impact upon him.

Of equal importance as a respite from Frank's New Jersey adolescence was the presence of Manhattan fifteen miles away, to which he would escape once or twice a month for a museum, theater, or foreign movie fix. The plays of Jean Genet appealed to him most as the dra-

facing page:
Frank Israel and Zelda Israel at Camp Tohone, 1956

Drawing, **split log cabin for Tohone camper, 1958**

matic counterparts of the existential Camus and Sartre he was reading at the same time. At the Eighth Street Playhouse in Greenwich Village, he savored Alain Resnais's artfully erotic *Hiroshima, Mon Amour* and the baroquely layered *Last Year at Marienbad*. Yet his favorite film, then and later, was Hiroshi Teshigahara's sensuous *Woman in the Dunes*. At MOMA, he was stunned by Picasso's *Guernica* and, as a result, wrote a school research paper on it and the Spanish Civil War. Such highbrow fare coexisted, of course, with a furtive love of middlebrow bathos, such as Herman Wouk's *Marjorie Morningstar*, the heroine of which epitomized the upper east side princess that every Jewish boy was supposed to want to marry.

Embracing New York in the 1950s also meant embracing architecture, which included Pennsylvania Station, where, in Vincent Scully's phrase, one "entered the city like a god." There was also the Deco skyscraper parade of the Chrysler, Empire State, and Rockefeller Center buildings. Because his doting father had observed architectural velleities in his childhood designs for puppet theaters and toy ranch houses, he took Frank once in the mid-1950s to see Gordon Bunshaft's much-heralded Lever House. The green glass was great, Israel later recalled, but, as he turned around, he was considerably more smitten by Mies and Johnson's Seagram Building under construction across Park Avenue.

In 1963, disappointed by rejections from Amherst and Princeton, Israel entered the University of Pennsylvania as a philosophy major. He recalled that his father, as he drove him down to Penn, said to him perceptively: "Now you're going to start enjoying your life." And, indeed, though he would later realize that his teenage years had been better than he knew, he agreed that college and the new worlds it opened were momentous in shaping and redirecting his life.

His first memorable experience at Penn was in pulling up the shade of his dormitory window and seeing the then-incredible profile of Louis Kahn's almost completed Richards Medical Center. He immediately became a Kahn devotee, a commitment which was confirmed after he wandered one day into a studio the architect was teaching with the engineers August Komendant and Robert Le Ricolais. It was being held at the top of the stairs of the Frank Furness Library (1891), another building that intrigued Israel as it had already fascinated Kahn and Robert Venturi. The dialogue between Kahn, his colleagues, and his students was mystical and seductive and evoked the relationship between architecture and poetry. It encouraged Israel to sit in on other design studios and to hang out at the Architecture School, where he was captivated especially by the energy and anxiety of the final reviews. This was something he could clearly relate to, and he changed his undergraduate major to architecture. He studied drawing with the artist Neil Welliver and took demanding design courses with Stanislawa Nowicki, widow of the architect Matthew Nowicki. He worked part-time as a model builder in Kahn's Philadelphia office and was rewarded for his devotion after a late-night charrette by being taken by the master to a Clint Eastwood movie.

In the middle 1960s, Penn was a lively place with a steady stream of interesting visitors. Among many important presentations, Israel later recalled that a particularly memorable one was Charles Moore's showing of the designs for his yet-to-be-built Sea Ranch. Still, for Israel, the most important part of his undergraduate education was the chance to audit a design theory course with Robert Venturi. Whereas he had been struck with the strange beauty of Kahn's Richards laboratories, he was equally impressed, on first encounter, with the beguiling "ugliness" of Venturi's mother's house (1964), a building which, as one got to know it, took on a new kind of beauty. It was painted green and had an oddly flat quality reminiscent of Warhol's contemporary paintings. The architect's red brick Guild House (1963) was shockingly symmetrical with decorative stringcourses and historical references that thumbed their noses at modernist purity. Venturi's work, then and later, Israel avers, "demands that you look at it again and again and teaches you how drawing, plan, and elevation relate to each other. The most important thing about Venturi at the time was that he gave young architects a reason to keep going. He persuaded us that small things — a dorky little house, a dumb restaurant — could be made into art." Venturi's *Complexity and Contradiction in Architecture*, published in 1966 by the Museum of Modern Art, confirmed and extended Israel's sense of Venturi's importance. When the author handed Israel a copy of the book, he reminded him that he should "not think *too* much about it; just read it and then get to work designing." With Venturi's encouragement, Israel wrote his senior thesis on Frank Furness's urbanism.

After graduating from Penn, the architect-to-be enrolled at Yale, but this was 1967 and the

6

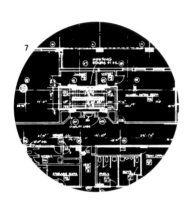
7

8

1 Still from *Horishima Mon Amour*
2 **Seagram Building, New York**
3 **View of Richards Medical Research Building from dormitories, University of Pennsylvania**
4 **Furness Library, University of Pennsylvania**
5 **Robert Venturi, Vanna Venturi House, Chestnut Hill,Pa.**
6 **Richard Weinstein, Bronfman House, Montreal**
7 **Giovanni Pasanella, *Detail, drawing*, P.S. 205, Bronx, N.Y.**
8 ***Detail*, church at Birnau, Bavaria**

school, like the nation, was in a tumult over the Vietnam War. Though he made important friendships with fellow students, he felt at loose ends emotionally, found New Haven depressing, and after one semester took a leave of absence and returned to New York, where he worked for one year with Gruzen and Partners, a well-known office. Despite the larger problems in the nation and the world, New York, in the later 1960s, was the most exciting place he had ever lived, and he consummated the love affair with the city he had begun in his teens. The art scene in Soho was becoming especially lively, and he hung out frequently at Andy Warhol's and Les Levine's bar, The Longview, near Union Square.

In the fall of 1968, because he wanted to stay in New York, he enrolled at Columbia, where he found much of the same creative, and destructive, turmoil he had known at Yale. Though he had always identified with left-of-center politics, he was considered "rightist" by his classmates because he chose to design buildings as student projects rather than write manifestoes. While he admired Romaldo Giurgola and worked part-time in his New York office, the Columbia teacher who most impressed Israel was the recently arrived Robert A.M. Stern. However much he might later differ with Stern's commitment to historicism, he appreciated his energy, passion, and *joie de vivre*, his loyal support of people he admired, and his willingness to push those people to fulfill their potential. Stern enlisted Israel's help in his then-controversial exhibition programs at the Architectural League of New York, where he also met Suzanne Stephens, then an editor at *Architectural Forum*, who would thenceforth play an equally supportive role as friend and critic, and was the first to publish Israel's work.

Israel, like many of his East Coast cohorts, also found stimulation during this period from Stern's ideological rival, Peter Eisenman, and his Institute for Architecture and Urban Studies. In an era of post-modernist ascendancy, the IAUS tended the simmering flame of modernism through a series of lectures, conferences, and publications. In the early 1970s, it and the Architectural League were the liveliest forums in the country for the discussion of contemporary architectural issues. Israel learned from them both.

From 1968 to 1970, while a student at Columbia, he worked part-time for Richard Weinstein, who, along with Jaquelin Robertson and Jonathan Barnett, formed Mayor John Lindsay's triad of architectural planners in the Manhattan-based Urban Design Group of the New York City Planning Commission. Like other mentors in his life at this time, Weinstein helped Israel shift his attention from the design of single buildings to the larger urban landscape. On the side, as well, Israel assisted Weinstein as a draftsman and model builder on the Bronfman House in Montreal, a building whose plan, massing, bowed frontality, and "violated" geometry, would influence Israel's later work. In both planning and architectural roles, he was impressed with the uniqueness of Weinstein's offbeat intelligence, which from then on would stimulate him toward new and unexpected ways of looking at things.

In 1971, after graduating from Columbia, Israel worked for Giovanni Pasanella Associates, extending the urban commitments he had developed with Weinstein by designing a school and low-cost housing in the Bronx. Pasanella also allowed him to accept his first independent commission, the constructivist/shingle–style Snell House in East Hampton (1973) for former staffers from old Camp Tohone. Suzanne Stephens published it in *Architectural Forum*, and Scully later included it in *The Shingle Style Today* (1974).

In 1973, Israel won the Rome Prize, a signal honor and a momentous event in his life. Jury members Philip Johnson and Robert Stern pushed for his selection, and he left New York for two heady years at the American Academy in Rome. There he pursued the usual mix of study, contemplation, drawing, travel, and socializing. The latter was especially rich for both his personal and professional future, particularly his association with Richard Meier, who was senior resident at the Academy. With Meier, architect Tim Vreeland, and historian Daniel Gregory, Frank went on a pilgrimage to Balthasar Neumann's Franconian churches — one of many European junkets that enriched his understanding of architecture and history. In Italy, he also deepened his appreciation of the Italian modernist Carlo Scarpa. He discussed Palladio with historian James Ackerman and explored Rome with classicist Bernard Frischer, but the association with Meier had the greatest effect on his architectural sensibility. Like Eisenman's Institute, which had championed modernist principles, Meier's sternly elegant, insistently white neo-modernism was for Israel a healthy antidote to the pull of postmodern eclecticism. He found the latter appealing in the hands of a master like Venturi, but he knew that postmodernism in its more supercilious derivations was already leading to a fatally fatuous scenography, a quality not totally absent in some of Israel's own early work.

The two years in Europe were indeed so satisfying that he almost dreaded returning to America, a fate that was in fact postponed by another fortuitous offer: the chance to work with architect/planner Jaquelin Robertson on the Shahestan Pahlavi project in Iran. It was a vast mixed-use scheme for the almost total rebuilding of a large section of central Teheran, including governmental, cultural, and commercial structures permeated by park-like open spaces. Israel was allowed a major role in the design. Robertson, with Llewelyn-Davies of London, had won the commission over an impressive field, including Louis Kahn and Kenzo Tange. Though delighted to be involved in such a major and exotic undertaking, as opposed to a more routine practice in the United States, Israel wondered when he stepped off the plane if he had made a mistake. "Teheran was such a dump," he recalled. "Only Jaque Robertson's charisma made it seem exciting again." Born in China to American diplomats, Robertson had developed a renowned sophistication in dealing with Westerners and non-Westerners alike. His dedication to the understanding of Persian culture, Israel observed, was an object lesson in how to adapt and to embrace a non-Eurocentric approach to architecture and life. Even though the subsequent fall of the shah doomed the project to oblivion, Israel reaped from the experience great personal and professional enrichment.

Returning to New York in 1977, he worked briefly for Robertson before accepting a call from UCLA to teach in its architecture program. He was encouraged to make the move by Philip Johnson, who argued that Los Angeles was becoming one of the most important cities for architecture of the late twentieth century. Though he had mixed feelings about leaving New York and adapting to the vastly different culture of LA, he stayed on to become a tenured professor at UCLA, to set up a practice in Los Angeles, and to become a confirmed Angeleno. The rest, as the saying goes, is history. Three factors helped in his rapid LA acclimatization: the region's rich architectural traditions, the film culture of Hollywood, and the presence of Frank Gehry as a mentor and model for dealing with the contemporary city in architectural terms.

The modernist that Israel had known best before moving to California was Richard Neutra, whom he admired in the same ways he did Gropius and Mies and the other giants of the International Style. Yet seeing the work in its Los Angeles setting persuaded him of the importance of Neutra's ethic and aesthetic of "the machine in the garden." From the strong dramatic lines of the Lovell House of 1929 to his simpler Westwood apartment complexes of the 1930s and 1940s, Neutra's work turned out to be better than Israel had expected. And this was even more true of Rudolph Schindler, whose Kings Road House (1922) sank deep into his psyche as he inhabited its garage as an early architectural studio. Schindler's "constructivist" use of cheap and starkly contrasting materials appealed to his own similarly developing tendencies, as they had earlier to the young Frank Gehry. Reference to Schindler's work, both direct and indirect, would appear in Israel's buildings of the late 1980s. It was in LA, moreover, that Israel finally succumbed to the magic of Frank Lloyd Wright, particularly to the details of his concrete block houses of the 1920s and the details and massing of his 1939 Sturges House in Brentwood. The latter had been supervised by Wright's Taliesin apprentice, John Lautner, whose own subsequent LA work would show significant traces of the master's late style. Lautner's prototype restaurants for the Googie fastfood chain, for example, marked a unique convergence of "high" and "low" art. The exaggerated layering of the metal Googie "pylons," so reminiscent of the work of Wright and of his son Lloyd, also prefigured many of Israel's favorite motifs of the 1990s — particularly evident in the Bright studio renovation.

Working with, and against, the tradition of Los Angeles modernism was the hot/cool glamor of Hollywood art direction, a world that had intrigued Israel since his teenage days at the Eighth Street Playhouse. While repelled, as an architect, by the one-dimensional artificiality of the "set," he was equally mesmerized by the cool bravado of the best art directors, whose ability to create a glittering, instant, even plausible "environment," contrasted starkly with the ploddingly slow building process of real-world architecture. Happily exploiting various Hollywood connections, while performing the slow duty of developing his own practice, Israel worked as the art director for Roger Vadim's *Night Games*. The Vadim picture, "set" in Los Angeles, was actually filmed in the Philippines because of the cheaper labor costs. Though he would continue to enjoy the glamor of Hollywood, the false-front ethos and the dirty politics syndrome forced him to withdraw as an active participant. "It's fun to be a voyeur in Hollywood," he noted, "so long as you can pull back and realize that you are not

9 Frank Gehry, Gehry House, Santa Monica
10 Jacquelin T. Robertson, *model*, Shahestan Pahlavi
11 Designs for Rodger Vadim's *Night Games*,
    Richard Sharah, makeup
12 *Model*, created for the film,
    Scenes from an Imaginary Movie

11

12

13

14

actually under its thumb." His affinity with the culture, however, has brought him some of his best commissions, including homes for Joel Grey and Robert Altman, and the studios for Propaganda and Limelight. "I understand that world," he avers, "and my clients there know they can communicate with me."

The most important figure, personally and professionally, in Israel's acculturation to Los Angeles and to architecture in the 1980s was undoubtedly Frank Gehry, whom he met through Philip Johnson, and who became as significant to him in this period as Robert Venturi had been in the 1960s. While Gehry acknowledged his debts to Venturi and to other architects of the postmodern critique, his deeper loyalty was to the modernist tradition, particularly its expressionist and constructivist legacies. Transcending historical affinities, however, was Gehry's instinctive artistic response to the larger context of his buildings, in this case the sprawl, chaos, ugliness, and the beauty of Los Angeles. Better than any architect in the city's long history, Gehry had expressed in a growing body of work both the comic and the tragic in LA's complex makeup. In his juxtaposed clusters of artfully collided forms, Gehry had found a perfect "take" on the city. "It took me a while to understand Gehry's work," Israel recalled, "though it was not as bewildering as Venturi's had been at first. LA was not easy for an Easterner with a formalist education to comprehend. Frank's work helped me to adjust to Los Angeles and to feel comfortable here. LA is all about juxtapositions and annexations — not unlike London."

Israel is certain that Gehry's understanding of Los Angeles and his talent for expressing it "reified Venturi's ideas better than Venturi's own work does. Frank has a gutsy, street corner bravado that Venturi writes about, but doesn't have. In fact, I suspect that Venturi envies Gehry and regrets that he hasn't had as much fun with his work as Frank has had." While Gehry's direct influence is evident in such Israel commissions as Propaganda Films and the Speedway Cafe, its indirect influences are even more important. "How to adapt, how to `add on' to a building and to a city," Israel confirms, "is the lesson of Gehry's that I've learned the best." His debts to the master also extend to his own younger contemporaries who are, like himself, frequently perceived as being in the Gehry orbit. Of several such architects who emerged in the 1980s, the most important to Israel is Morphosis, particularly with their Lawrence House, Redondo Beach, 72 Market Street in Venice, the Cancer Treatment Center at Cedars-Sinai Hospital, and the nearby Salick highrise. "Gehry thinks I unconsciously emulate Morphosis," Israel observes, "but I would say that the major connection is our common debt to Gehry, our love of 'violated' geometry, and our admiration of Carlo Scarpa. I believe that through all of this, my own voice is beginning to emerge."

To anyone who knows the work and can track the orbit of an architectural takeoff, the fact that Frank Israel is finding his voice is becoming increasingly clear.

Thomas S. Hines teaches cultural and architectural history at UCLA. His books include Burnham of Chicago: Architect and Planner *and* Richard Neutra and the Search for Modern Architecture.

---

notes

1 This essay was based on seven hours of taped interviews with Frank Israel on August 21, 1991, as well as more informal conversations with Frank Gehry, Richard Weinstein, Mildred Friedman, Suzanne Stephens, Sylvia Lavin, and others. It also drew from the articles on Israel cited in the bibliography.

ARANGO-BERRY
F.D. ISRAEL
BEV. HILLS
RESIDENCE

index of buildings and projects

Projects discussed in this book are noted with a symbol ⌐

buildings

Snell House ⌐
Amagansett, Long Island, New York
1973

Christiaan Studio
Singel Canal, Amsterdam
1977

Christiaan Hair Salon
Singel Canal, Amsterdam
1978

Golden Harvest
Productions, Goldwyn Studios
Los Angeles, California
1978

Robert Abel Associates
Hollywood, California
1978

Night Games **Set**
Manila, Phillipines
1979

Paramount Sets
Hollywood, California
1979-1982

Joel Grey-Jo Wilder House
Brentwood, California
1980

Gordon Residence
Pacific Palisades, California
1982

Nightfall **Sets**
Venice, California
1981

Mid-Ocean Motion Pictures
Los Angeles, California
1980-92

Gillette Studio ⌐
New York, New York
1980-1982

Information International, Inc.
Los Angeles, California
1982

Sabatino Residence
Hollywood, California
1982

MAGI
(The Mathematical Applications Group,Inc.)
Santa Monica, California
1982

Mc Call-Coppola Film Fair
Studio City, California
1982

Rich Apartment
Los Angeles, California
1984

Pallette Interior
Hollywood, California
1984

Kiefer Residence
Pacific Palisades, California
1984

Houseman Residence
Brentwood, California
1984

Wilshire Boulevard Apartment
Los Angeles, California
1984

Miller Office
West Hollywood, California
1984

Lerner-Wilder-La Brea
Los Angeles, California
1984

Jules Stein Residence
Los Angeles, California
1985

Arkush Residence
Studio City, California
1985

Honey Springs Country Club *(interiors)*
San Diego, California
1985

Certified Coatings Company
Los Angeles, California
1986

Semel Residence
Los Angeles, California
1985

Semel Beach House
Malibu, California
1985

UCLA Installation I
Westwood, California
1987

Altman House ⌐
Malibu, California
1988

Harris Residence
Los Angeles, California
1987-1988

Klein Residence
Bel Air, California
1988

Lamy-Newton Pavilion ⌐
Hancock Park, California
1988

Propaganda Films
Hollywood, California
1988

Architecture Tomorrow,
A Walker Art Center Exhibit
Minneapolis, Minnesota
Oct. 1988-Jan. 1989

Arango-Berry House
Summitridge, California
1989

Randy and Dianne Roberts House
Hollywood, California
1989

Bright and Associates
Venice, California
1991

Art Pavilion
Beverly Hills, California
1991

Limelight Productions
Los Angeles, California
1991

Virgin Records
Beverly Hills, California
1991

Goldberg-Bean House
Hollywood, California
1991

Tisch-Avnet
Culver City, California
1991

Borman House *(interiors)*
Malibu, California
1990

UCLA Installation II
Westwood, California
1991

Speedway Cafe
Venice, California
1991

Divine Design Pavilion
Santa Monica, California
1991

projects

Floating Hotel
New York, New York
1973

Pool House for Audrey Hepburn
Rome, Italy
1974

Roman Pool House
Rome, Italy
1974

Pool House
Amagansett, Long Island, New York
1974

Villa San Miniatelli
Braciano, Italy
1975

Cenotaph for Henry James
Rome, Italy
1975

Bamboo Bungalow
Manila, Philippines
1978

Clark House
Hollywood, California
1980

Bellisle House
Santa Barbara, California
1980

West Hollywood Club
West Hollywood, California
1982

Arrow House
Lake Arrowhead, California
1984

John Rich Residence
Truesdale, California
1986

Hard Rock Hotel
Las Vegas, Nevada
1987

Bombyk House
Los Angeles, California
1987

Mid-Atlantic Toyota
Glen Burnie, Maryland
1988

Arlene and Bill Gerber House
Westwood, California
1989

Gateway for Cemetery at Crystal Cathedral
London, England
1989

East Hampton Airlines Terminal
East Hampton, New York
1990

John Tesh House
Mar Vista, California
1991

The New England Holocaust Memorial
Boston, Massachusetts
1991

Carol and Jerry Isenberg House
Montecito, California
1991

Raznick House
Hollywood Hills, California
1991

Kaplan House
Malibu, California
1991

UCLA Southern Regional Library
Westwood, California
1991

Sydney and Susan Baldwin House
Venice, California
1992

Woo Pavilion
Silverlake, California
1992

Hague House
The Hague, The Netherlands
1992

Bunka Shutter
and the New Industrial City
Tokyo, Japan
1992

biography

Born in New York City in 1945, Franklin Israel received his education at the University of Pennsylvania, Yale, and Columbia. He was awarded The Rome Prize in Architecture in 1973. Currently, he is an Associate Professor in the School of Architecture and Urban Planning at the University of California, Los Angeles, and was a Visiting Professor at Harvard University's Graduate School of Design in 1989–1990. He has lectured at Columbia, Harvard, Berkeley, The Graham Foundation in Chicago, and numerous institutions in America and abroad.

The firm of Franklin D. Israel Design Associates has been in existence since 1983. Prior to that, Israel worked with Giovanni Pasanella in New York, and Llewelyn-Davies, Weeks, Forestier-Walker and Bor in London and Teheran. He also has been involved in several small design partnerships working on projects in New York and Los Angeles, and Europe. From 1978 to 1979 he served as an art director at Paramount Pictures, where he worked on film projects in Los Angeles, China, and the Philippines.

Recent projects by his firm include offices for Propaganda Films in Hollywood, Tisch-Avnet Productions in Los Angeles, Bright and Associates in Venice, and Virgin Records in Beverly Hills. Residential work includes a Malibu beach house for Mr. and Mrs. Robert Altman, a living and working studio in New York for photographer Rick Gillette, and the Los Angeles home of artist Richard Newton and designer Michele Lamy. Articles on his work have been published in *Lotus, Architectural Digest, Architectural Review, Progressive Architecture, Architectural Record, The New York Times,* and other journals and magazines in this country and abroad.

In the fall of 1989 he mounted an exhibition at The Walker Art Center entitled "Six Mementos for the Next Millennium." This show was the first in the series "Architecture Tomorrow." It traveled to San Francisco's Museum of Modern Art and then to the Murray Feldman Gallery at the Pacific Design Center in Los Angeles.

exhibits

The Architect's Sketchbook: Current Practices
Canadian Centre for Architecture, Montreal
1992

Architect's office
Frank Israel Design Associates
UCLA Graduate School of Architecture and
Urban Planning, Los Angeles
1992

New Corporate Interiors: Los Angeles
Kimball International, Los Angeles
1991

Les Architectes Plasticiens
Saddock and Uzzan Gallery, Paris
1991

Drawings
The Getty Center, Santa Monica
1990–1991

From Cities Within
American Institute of Architects, Dallas
1990

Westweek Annual Exhibition
Los Angeles
1989

New Materials Steelcase Exhibit
Murray Feldman Gallery, Los Angeles
1988
IDCA, New York City
1989

Architecture Tomorrow: Franklin D. Israel
Walker Art Center, Minneapolis;
San Francisco Museum of Modern Art;
Murray Feldman Gallery, Los Angeles
1988–1989

Forty Under 40 Design Exhibition
New York City, Chicago, Cincinnati, Houston
1987

Three Projects
Perloff Hall, University of California, Los Angeles
1987

The Light I Like
California Polytechnic Institute
San Luis Obispo
1984

Los Angeles Now
Architectural Association, London
1983

Pentagon House
School of Architecture and Urban Planning,
University of California, Los Angeles
1983

The California Condition
La Jolla Museum of Art, La Jolla
1982

Visiting Artists
University of Idaho, Moscow, Idaho
1982

Room, Window, Furniture
The Cooper Union, New York City
1981–82
GA Gallery, Tokyo
1983

The Chicago Tribune Competition Exhibition
Chicago, Syracuse, La Jolla
1980–1981

Towards a More Modern Architecture
Young Architects Art Gallery,
Yale University, New Haven
1980

American Architectural Alternatives
London, Paris, Amsterdam, Zurich, Rome,
and Madrid
1979–1980

Drawing Towards a More Modern Architecture
Otis Art Gallery, Los Angeles
1978

Cenotaph to Henry James
The Drawing Center, New York City
1978

Alternative Beauborg
School of Architecture and Urban Planning,
University of California, Los Angeles
1977

Projects Built and Not
ART NET, London
1976

Cenotaph to Henry James
American Academy in Rome Annual Exhibit, Rome
1975

Pool Houses and Hotel
American Academy in Rome Annual Exhibit, Rome
1974

selected bibliography

Writings by Frank Israel

"Montage, Collage, and Broken Narrative." *Critical Architecture*, October 1989, pp. 14–19.

"The 6th Street House." *Representation Via 9*, 1988, pp. 26–27.

"Westside Pavilion Reviewed." *L.A. Architect*, February 1986.

"The Decorator's World: A World Apart From Ours." *Crit 14*, J.I.A.E Journal, Fall 1984, pp. 66–67.

"The Architecture of Helmut Jahn." *G.Q.*, September 1983.

"L.A. Physique." *G.Q.*, June 1983.

"Casa di Sabbia." *AD: Architectural Digest Italia*, Vol. 2, No. 16, September 1982, pp. 102–109, 194.

"Venice Biennale Reviewed." *L.A. Architect*, August 1982.

"Beverly Center Reviewed." *L.A. Architect*, July 1982, p. 2.

"From Out of Nowhere: Cities and City Planners." *G.Q.*, June 1982, p. 40.

"Arata Isozaki's Cubic Feats." *G.Q.*, March 1982, p. 58.

"Piecing The Puzzle That's Downtown L.A." *G.Q.*, January 1982, pp. 59, 62.

"Frank O. Gehry's California Framework." *G.Q.*, December 1981, p. 45.

"The Passion of L.A.'s Joan of Art." *G.Q.*, September 1981, p. 52.

"Moore Builds Odes To The Past." *G.Q.*, August 1981, p. 44.

"On The (Melrose) Road." *Progressive Architecture*, September 1981, pp. 168–172.

"Orient Express: The China Club." *Progressive Architecture*, September 1981, pp. 156–158.

"Artist's Dialogue: Joe Goode." *Architectural Digest*, September 1981, pp. 64, 68, 72, 74.

"Georgia O'Keefe." *Architectural Digest*, Vol. 38, No. 7, July 1981, pp. 76–86, 136, 138.

"In Small Compass: An Elegant Mastery of Spacial Limitations." *Architectural Digest*. Vol. 37, No. 10, December 1980, pp. 114–121.

"William Morgan." *Architectural Digest*, Vol. 36, No. 10, December 1979, pp. 86–91.

"Architecture: Neil Astle." *Architectural Digest*, Vol. 35, No. 6, July/August 1978, pp. 66–73.

"Architecture: Paul Rudolph." *Architectural Digest*, Vol. 35, No. 5, June 1978, pp. 90–99.

"Architecture: E. Fay Jones." *Architectural Digest*, Vol. 37, No. 8, October 1978, pp. 76–81.

"Earls Court Elegance." *Progressive Architecture*, Vol. 58, No. 9, September 1977, pp. 90–93.

"In the Nature of Fake Materials." *Progressive Architecture*, Vol. 58, No. 9, September 1977, pp. 90–93.

"Frank Israel Speaks: The Venice Biennale." *RIBA Journal*, November 1976, p. 478.

"Accommodating Moore." *L'Architecture D'Aujour D'Hui*, April/May 1976.

"Con Moore e Meier negli anni '70." *Controspazio*, September 1975, pp. 35–37.

"A East Hampton." *Ville Giardini*, December 1974.

Writings on Frank Israel

1992

Anderton, Frances. "Gloom Time L.A." *L.A. Architect*, February 1992, p. 5.

———. "Material World." *Architecture Magazine*, January 1992, pp. 31–43.

Betsky, Aaron. "Art Barn." *Architectural Record*, February 1992, pp. 66–73.

Reese, Carol McMichael. "The Architect's Sketchbook: Current Practices," February 1992, pp. 20–21.

Vogel, Angeline. "Style! Vigor! Action!" *Designer's West*, January 1992, pp. 78–83.

1991

Anderton, Frances. "Bright Ideals." *Architectural Review*, March 1991, pp. 57–60.

"Arango-Berry Residence." *GA Houses*, Vol. 30, February 1991.

Betsky, Aaron. "Simple Shells Often Conceal Rich Interiors." *The Los Angeles Times*, Westside Section, July 18, 1991, p. J2.

Beylerian, George M., and Jeffrey J. Osborne. *Mondo Materialis: Materials and Ideas for the Future* (New York: Harry N. Abrams, Inc. for Steelcase Design Partnership, 1990), p. 120.

"The Dream Storehouse," Propaganda Films Offices, Hollywood A & V 32 1991, pp. 68–71.

Favro, Diane, and Jeffrey Chusid. "Six Mementos for the Next Millenium." *Design Quarterly*, No. 152, 1991, pp. 7–14.

"Gillette Studio, New York." *Lotus International*, March 1991, p. 46.

Guralnick, Margot. "The Producers." *House and Garden*, July 1991.

"Kaplan House and Goldberg-Bean House." *GA Houses*, Vol. 31, 1991, pp. 74–77.

"Now & Then." *Vogue*, January 1991, pp. 186–191, 219.

"Venice: Re-Design für Charles Eames." *Ambiente*, Vol. 7/8, August 1991, p. 14.

1990

Bagnall, Diana. "Strictly Speaking." *Australian Vogue Living*, August 1990, pp. 82–83, 151.

Betsky, Aaron. "Ranchburger Deluxe." *Metropolitan Home*, October 1990, pp. 137–140.

———. "Steel and Stone: Los Angeles Architect Frank Israel on the Cutting Edge." *W Magazine*, October 15–22, 1990.

———. "Dreams of Israel." *Architectural Review*, January 1990, pp. 53–57.

Boissiere, Olivier. "Franklin D. Israel, Une Architecture Savant." *L'Architecture D'Aujourd'hui*, No. 271, October 1990, pp. 145–163.

Dixon, John Morris. "Within a Hallowed Shell." *Progressive Architecture*, September 1990, pp. 96–102.

Dungan, Sebastian. "Frank Israel: From Within." *Venice: The Magazine*, Vol. 2, No. 4, July 1990, p. 68.

Favro, Diane, and Jeffrey Chusid. "Franklin D. Israel: Due Case Unifamiliari a Los Angeles." *Domus*, No. 719, September 1990, pp. 74–81.

"Frank Israel." *Architecture*, December 1990, p. 28.

"Frank Israel: Escenografias Fragmentarias." *Arquitectura & Construccion*, May 16, 1990.

Lavin, Sylvia. "Creativity Begets Creativity." *Designer's West*, September 1990, pp. 68–75.

Moore, Rowan. "Complexity and Contradiction." *Blueprint*, May 1990, pp. 41–47.

Mulard, Claudine. "Los Angeles Une Ville Sous Influence." *City Magazine*, No. 65, November, 1990, pp. 106–113.

Muschamp, Herbert. "Ground Up." *Artforum*, October 1990, pp. 31–33.

Robinson, Gaile. "Michele Lamy Somehow Knits it all Together." *The Los Angeles Times*, November 1990, pp. E1, E5.

Stengel, Richard. "The Best of Design." *Time*, December 31, 1990, p. 48.

Stephens, Suzanne. "Decaying Venice Veneer For a Corporate Identity." *The New York Times*, Currents, June 6, 1990.

Vogel, Carol. "Home on the Range." *The New York Times Magazine*, April 22, 1990, pp. 28–31.

Webb, Michael. "901." *LA Style*, September 1990, pp. 198–201.

Whiteson, Leon. "Industrial Strength Design Studio Pays Homage to Past." *The Los Angeles Times*, April 16, 1990, p. E4.

———. "Angeleno Abstraction." *Architecture*, March 1990.

1989

"89 for 89." *The Los Angeles Times Magazine*, Vol. V, No. 1, January 1, 1989, p. 6.

Betsky, Aaron. "Frank Israel in Charette." *Inland Architecture*, January-February 1989, pp. 17–18.

Dietsch, Deborah K. "With Due Respect," "Mythic Proportions," and "Different Strokes." *Architectural Record*, April 1989, pp. 65–68.

Goldberger, Paul. "The Quest for Comfort." *The New York Times Home Magazine*, Part 2, October 15, 1989, pp. 36–38.

———. "Architecture: Franklin D. Israel, Kathryn and Robert Altman's Residence." *Architectural Digest*, July 1989, pp. 120–125, 180.

———. "Taking the Pulse of New American Architecture." *The New York Times*, Home Section, January 1, 1989, p. H30.

"Letters from Los Angeles." *Blueprint*, February 1989, p. 14.

Rand, G. "Film Studio Swings With Its Users." *Architecture*, June 1989, pp. 56–59.

Schlinke, Britton. "Under the Influence." *Art Week*, Vol. 20, No. 15, April 15, 1989, p. 3.

Suisman, Doug. "A Prairie Home Cousanguine." *L.A. Architect*, January 1989, pp. 8–9.

Vécsey, Esther. "The House that Frank Built." *The Daily Californian*, April 5, 1989.

Viladas, Pilar. "California Modern." *House and Garden*, June 1989, pp. 28–30.

Whiteson, Leon. "Now Playing: Avant-Garde Movie 'Boutiques.'" *The Los Angeles Times*, Part V, May 19, 1989, pp. 1, 4.

Wright, Bruce N. "Frank Israel at Walker." *Progressive Architecture*, January 1989.

1988

Whiteson, Leon. "Frank Israel: Designs With a Sense of Irony." *The Los Angeles Times*, Part V, November 3, 1988, pp. 1, 16.

1987

Anderton, Frances. "New Light on L.A., Frank Israel: A House In The Hollywood Hills." *Architectural Review*, No. 1090, December 1987, pp. 61–62.

Nordwind, Richard. "Cornering of L.A.'s Markets." *Los Angeles Herald Examiner*, June 1987.

Viladas, Pilar. "In Progress: Mid-Atlantic Toyota Distributors, Inc." *Progressive Architecture*, August 1987, p. 39.

Whiteson, Leon. "Building a Career In Movies." *Los Angeles Herald Examiner*, July 1987.

1986

"The Gillette Studio and New Barragan." *Architecture und Wohnen*, February 1986, pp. 18–22.

Littlejohn, David. "Architect: The Life and Work of Charles W. Moore." *Design Book Review*, Fall 1986.

McNair, Andrew. "Forty Under Forty—The New Generation of Designers." *Interiors Magazine*, September 1986, pp. 149, 176.

Stephens, Suzanne. "More Than Skin Deep." *House and Garden*, January 1986, pp. 80–88, 177.

Vogel, Carol. "Lean, Clean Mies Gets 2nd Look." *Chicago Tribune*, Home Section 15, February 23, 1986, pp. 2–3.

1985

Gandee, Charles. "Great Performances." *Architectural Record*, Mid-September 1985, p. 87.

Takei, Satoshi. "Interior Advantage." *Brutus*, January 1985, pp. 162–163.

"Young American Architects." *Space Design*, September 1985.

1984

Lerup, Lars. "Feast For The Senses." *Architectural Digest*, November, 1984, p. 132.

1983

Chase, John. "The Garret, The Boardroom and The Amusement Park." *Journal, A Contemporary Art Magazine*, The Los Angeles Institute of Contemporary Art, Spring 1983, pp. 21–27.

Giovannini, Joseph. "California Architects at La Jolla." *Skyline*, January 1983, p. 24.

Goldstein, Barbara. "Frank Israel." *SAUP Magazine*, Winter 1983, pp. 14–19.

Goldstein, Barbara, and Peter Cook. *Los Angeles Now*. Catalogue for exhibition at the Architectural Association, London, 1983.

"House With a Balcony." *Sunset Magazine*, August 1983.

1982

California Condition—A Pregnant Architecture. Exhibit catalogue. (La Jolla: La Jolla Museum of Art, 1982) pp. 49–53.

"The California Condition." *Architecture California*, December 1982.

"California." *Space Design*, August 1982.

Giovannini, Joseph. "The California Condition." *Los Angeles Herald Examiner*, December 1982.

Ianco-Starrels, Josine. "Our Risky Style in Architecture." *The Los Angeles Times*, November 1982.

Oliver, Richard. "Emerging Voices." *Skyline*, May 1982, pp. 10–13.

1981

Phillips, Eleanor. "A Little Grey House In The West." *Vogue*, July 1981.

Williams, Tod, and Ricardo Scofidio. *Window Room Furniture* (New York: Rizzoli Press, 1981), p. 39.

1980

Pennington, Ron. "Night Games." *The Hollywood Reporter*, April 30, 1980.

Scofidio, Richard "American Architecture Alternatives." Graham Foundation for Advanced Studies in The Fine Arts, 1980.

Tigerman, Stanley. *Late Entries to the Chicago Tribune Tower Competition, Volume II* (New York: Rizzoli International Publications, Inc., 1980), p. 40.

1978

Allen, Gerald, and Dale Furman. "A Guide to Architect Designed Houses." *Town & Country*, September 1978.

Ranalli, George. *Young Architects* (New Haven: Yale University Press, 1978), p. 10.

1977

Chapman, Miles. "The Shah's New Town." *Harper's*, April 1977, pp. 170–171.

Stern, Robert A.M. "40 Under 40." *A&U*, January 1977, p. 110.

———. "America Now: Drawing Towards a More Modern Architecture." *Architectural Design*, June 1977, pp. 381, 431.

1976

Robertson, J.T. "Shahestan Pahlavi." *RIBA Journal*, November 1976.

1975

Ercolani, Giampaolo. "Frank Israel: Una Ricerca Architettonica Delle Giovani Generazioni." *Contraspazio*, September 1975, pp. 30–34.

Hart, John. "At The Academy." Review of the annual show at the American Academy in Rome. *Daily American*, Rome, Italy, June 11, 1975.

1974

Scully, Vincent. *The Shingle Style Revisited—A Historian's Revenge* (New York: George Braziller, Inc., 1974), p. 23.

office staff

Associates

Barbara Callas
Annie Chu
Jeffrey N. Chusid
Mitchell DeJarnet
Paul Fortune
Danelle Guthrie
Yoichiro Hakomori
Milena Iancovici Murdoch
Thomas A. Rael
H. Seth Rosenthal
Steven S. Shortridge

Staff

Amy Alper
Felix Ang
David Applebaum
Mel Bernstein
Andre Bilokur
Pamela S. Birkel
Neal Borsuk
Tomaso Bradshaw
Ross Brennan
Tom Buresh
Cynthia Carlson
Chuck Conner
Isabelle Coulet
Jay Deguchi
Christopher Duncan
Craig Dykers
Rob Flock
Christian Garnett
Sara Garnett
Bettina Gehlen
Rick Gooding
Harold L. Graham
Sari A. Grenell
James R. Harlan
Joseph L. Holsen
Gary Hulton
David N. Jensen
Doris Jew

Christoph Kapeller
Danny Kaplan
Pongsatorn Kawdee
Doug Keekan
Robert Knight
Aimee Knowlton
Adam R. Koffman
Kamal Kozah
Michael Larice
Michael Lee
Nina Lesser
Dwain Lind
Christian B. Lynch
Myung S. Moon
Eric Morris
William Molthen
Kevin O'Brien
Carol O'Leary
Brendan J. O'Neill
Morton Olrik
Kevin Oreck
C. Alejandro Ortiz
Carol Patterson
Michael C. Poris
Daniel B. Ross
Faith Rosenblatt
Rob Rosenblatt
Glenda D. Rovello
Lindy Roy
Leslie Shapiro
James W. Simeo
Richard Stoner
Matthew F. Tapia
Jim Chang Tsai
Elizabeth Villalba
Michael Volk
Linda L. Wehbi
Alexander H. Whang
Dennis Whelan
Julian Yip
George Yu

and given half a chance, nature takes over again